Cambridge Ele

C000258102

Elements in New Religious [
edited by
Rebecca Moore
San Diego State University
Founding Editor
James R. Lewis
Wuhan University

FROM RADICAL JESUS PEOPLE TO VIRTUAL RELIGION

The Family International

Claire Borowik

CAMBRIDGE
UNIVERSITY PRESS

Shaftesbury Road, Cambridge CB2 8EA, United Kingdom

One Liberty Plaza, 20th Floor, New York, NY 10006, USA

477 Williamstown Road, Port Melbourne, VIC 3207, Australia

314–321, 3rd Floor, Plot 3, Splendor Forum, Jasola District Centre,
New Delhi – 110025, India

103 Penang Road, #05–06/07, Visioncrest Commercial, Singapore 238467

Cambridge University Press is part of Cambridge University Press & Assessment,
a department of the University of Cambridge.

We share the University's mission to contribute to society through the pursuit of
education, learning and research at the highest international levels of excellence.

www.cambridge.org
Information on this title: www.cambridge.org/9781009017602

DOI: 10.1017/9781009037990

First published 2023

A catalogue record for this publication is available from the British Library.

ISBN 978-1-009-01760-2 Paperback
ISSN 2635-232X (online)
ISSN 2635-2311 (print)

From Radical Jesus People to Virtual Religion

The Family International

Elements in New Religious Movements

DOI: 10.1017/9781009037990
First published online: January 2023

Claire Borowik

Author for correspondence: Claire Borowik, claire.borowik@gmail.com

Abstract: The Family International (formerly the Children of God) emerged from the radical fringe of the Jesus People Movement in the late 1960s to establish a new religious movement with communities in ninety countries. Characterized from its early days by controversy due to its unconventional version of Christianity, countercultural practices, and high level of tension with society, the Family International created a communal society that endured for four decades. The movement's reinvention in 2010 as an online community offers insights into the dynamic nature of new religious movements, as they strategically adapt to evolving social contexts and emergent issues, and the negotiations of belief and identity this may entail. The Family International's transformation from a radical communal movement to a deradicalized virtual community highlights the novel challenges alternative religions may face in entering the mainstream and attaining legitimacy within the increasingly globalized context of online information dissemination in virtual spaces.

Keywords: The Family International, Children of God, communal living, Endtime, religion online, organizational transformation

ISBNs: 9781009017602 (PB), 9781009037990 (OC)
ISSNs: 2635-232X (online), 2635-2311 (print)

Contents

Introduction

The Children of God (COG) emerged from the radical fringe of the Jesus People Movement in the late 1960s to establish a new religious movement with a presence in more than ninety countries and a transnational culture guided by prophetic revelation. Characterized by its unconventional version of Christianity, countercultural practices, and high degree of tension with society, the movement's worldview was constructed as a "radically Christian response to culture" (Niebuhr 1951: 65–76), centered in its vision of first-century Christian communalism and rejection of contemporary society. From its beginnings in California to its evolution into an international new religious movement with 10,000 members, the COG's evangelical purpose galvanized its members to missionize around the globe with its unique presentation of the Gospel message. The movement produced a vibrant subculture and was prolific in the creation of original musical and multimedia productions, artwork, and in-house publications for evangelism, community engagement, and charitable works in thirty languages.

The Children of God (later known as the Family and currently the Family International) developed a communal society that endured for forty-two years despite daunting challenges and financial scarcity, sustained by a common belief system, lifestyle, and shared rituals. The Family demonstrated a considerable degree of resourcefulness and resilience in responding to emergent issues, delayed millennial expectations, and evolving contexts within the movement, as well as changes to the surrounding sociocultural environment. Members proved adept at acclimating to a diversity of local customs and languages and recruiting new members from nearly 100 nationalities while sustaining the movement's social structure and culture. The cohesion and organizational stability of the COG's communal model was instrumental for the movement's longevity and sustainability, and the development of a coherent way of life despite continuous controversy and opposition.

The Family's history has been punctuated by periodic reorganizations and redirections, referred to internally as "revolutions," documented in nearly 4,000 writings published by the movement's leadership from 1968 to 2010. Recurrent trends of experimentation, accommodation, adaptation, and reorganization resulted in a continuous remapping of its organizational structure and the creation of a milieu of change and innovation, as Melton noted:

> If there has been any persistent truth about the Family during its several decades of existence, it has been its almost annual ability to introduce novelty and change into the routine into which its members would otherwise fall. This novelty makes the Family interesting to scholars, confounds its critics, and prevents even the most careful observers from predicting its future. (Melton 1997: 61–62)

In 2010, an unprecedented organizational restructuring, dubbed "the Reboot," introduced radical transformation to virtually every aspect of the movement's belief system and communal lifestyle, and ultimately redefined the course of its history. In the aftermath of the Reboot's disassembling of the movement's organizational structure and dismantling of the communal homes, the Family International (TFI) organically evolved into an amorphous virtual community with little formal structure beyond its online presence. The revisionism introduced at the Reboot, in particular the distancing from controversial doctrines and practices, resulted in unforeseen post-Reboot renegotiations of the movement's worldview and identity. In the absence of TFI's communal society model, previously pivotal to the maintenance of a unified subculture and shared identity, the post-Reboot TFI has faced challenges in reconstructing community cohesion and recapturing the sense of collective purpose and belonging that previously characterized the movement.

Considering that TFI has embarked on what arguably may be the final chapter of its lifecycle in its current reconfiguration as an online religion, this Element will explore the movement's history, culture, doctrinal innovations, heterodox practices, controversies, and post-Reboot digital transformation. The complexity of TFI's history as a constantly evolving movement with three generations, coupled with the vast diversity in members' experiences and the shroud of controversy that continues to surround it, render it a challenging task to construct a narrative that will provide an adequate depiction of the movement and its members. The Family International's journey from the social construction of a unique microcosmic religious society to its metamorphosis as a virtual networked community offers insights into the innovative and dynamic nature of new religions and their ability to strategically adapt their beliefs and practices to accommodate changing cultural contexts. Its history also highlights the novel challenges new religions may face in mainstreaming religious belief and practice and attempting to attain legitimacy within the increasingly globalized context of digital information technologies and virtual spaces.

1 From the Children of God to the Family International: A Historical Overview

Born in the historical moment of the "cultural collision of the holiness movement and the psychedelic movement" of the late 1960s (Bainbridge 2002: 170), the Children of God emerged as a millenarian, antiestablishment communal movement. Initially an integral part of the Jesus People, the movement's adoption of unconventional beliefs and counterculture ideologies placed it on the margins of the larger movement early on. The COG's denunciation of the socioeconomic, cultural, and religious mainstream, and its communal lifestyle, unconventional doctrines, and heterodox sexual practices gave rise to opposition from hostile media, anticult organizations, mainstream Christianity, and law enforcement. An evolving array of new factors and issues required innovation and accommodation – notably the birth of a second (and later a third) generation of children, opposition and government interventions, the aging of the first generation, and the ongoing challenges of a complex communal lifestyle and financial precarity. The movement proved creative in overcoming adversity and responding adaptively to emergent internal and external exigencies, demonstrating what Bainbridge referred to as "a remarkable capacity for constant revolution" (Bainbridge 2002: 172). This section describes the early history of the COG, the evolution of its organizational framework, the movement's global dispersion, and the oppositional forces it has faced as a religious movement in high tension with the social milieu.

Early History

The Children of God had its genesis amid the turmoil of the 1960s in the United States, from which emerged a diverse array of new religious and social movements, characterized by the commitment of their largely youthful adherents, eclectic belief systems, and controversy. Tipton proposed that the turn from the psychedelic hip culture of the 1960s to alternative religions toward the end of the decade was precipitated to some extent by the "atmosphere of disappointment and depression" the counterculture youth experienced as the hippie movement waned and failed to deliver (Tipton 1982: 30). Alternative religions offered a means to synthesize cherished elements of the counterculture and its expressive and experiential ideals with purpose, direction, and authority. The most significant religious manifestation of the period arguably was the Jesus People Movement, which despite its relatively short lifespan (late 1960s to late 1970s) had a lasting impact on evangelical worship, music, and outreach, and profoundly reshaped evangelical culture (Eskridge 2013: 266–84; MacDonald & Stetzer 2020). The Jesus People Movement, described by Drakeford as "a strange shotgun marriage of conservative religion and a rebellious counterculture," gave rise to numerous communal groups in the late 1960s, the largest, and conceivably most controversial, of which was the COG (Drakeford 1972: 36; Miller 1999: 96). Founded by David Berg (1919–94), his wife Jane, and their four adult children in Huntington Beach, California, the COG was deemed the fastest growing movement to emerge from the Jesus People, with the greatest stability and organizational rationality (Enroth et al. 1972: 22; Davis & Richardson 1976: 338–39). The COG was also one of the few offshoots of the

Jesus People Movement that evolved into a new religious movement rather than being absorbed into denominational evangelicalism, and would outlive most of its counterparts by decades (Eskridge 2013: 5, 208).

David Berg hailed from an evangelical background as the son of Hjalmer Berg (1884–1964), an evangelist and later professor at Westmont College in Santa Barbara, and Virginia Brandt Berg (1886–1968), an evangelist and revivalist for the Christian and Missionary Church Alliance. Virginia's father, John Lincoln Brandt (1860–1946), was an itinerant preacher and author in the Alexander Campbell Restoration Movement of the Disciples of Christ. Virginia was a prominent radio evangelist and hosted a popular radio program, *Meditation Moments*, which aired for fifteen years in the 1930s and 1940s. Berg accompanied his mother in her ministry as a traveling evangelist through-out his early years, until he assumed a pastorate with the Christian and Missionary Alliance in 1948 at a small church in Arizona. According to Berg, the church's board deemed his teachings to be too radical, resulting in an acrimonious parting in 1951, to which Berg attributed the genesis of his disenchantment with institutional Christianity (Berg 1972c). He subsequently attended college briefly, where he was exposed to socialism and communism, which, according to his memoirs, he rejected as political systems while em-bracing the concept of a Christian version of socialism (Berg 1972c). After a short period of employment as a schoolteacher, Berg worked thirteen years for Fred Jordan, a fundamentalist Southern evangelist who produced *Church in the Home*, a radio and television program. Berg left Jordan's employ in 1967 to engage in itinerant evangelism with his wife and four children. In 1968, in response to an appeal from his elderly mother to evangelize the hippies congre-gating in Southern California, Berg and his family relocated to Huntington Beach, California.

By March 1968, Berg and the Teens for Christ, as they were initially known, had taken over the Light Club coffeehouse previously run by Pentecostal preacher Dave Wilkerson's Teen Challenge ministry. Early accounts portray the Teens for Christ as conservative young people ill-equipped to relate to the counterculture hippie youth (Wallis 1981: 99; Eskridge 2013: 64–65). They subsequently adopted the long hair, beards, and informal clothing of the unchurched counter-culture youth they sought to reach, and their evangelization on the beaches and the streets, coupled with the offer of free food and music at the Light Club, began to attract youths. Berg's teachings at the Light Club became radical and anti-establishment early on with his "declaration of revolution" in September 1968, in which he excoriated the social, political, and economic mainstream, collectively referred to as the "System," and institutional Christianity, and deemed education "the greatest enemy of civilisation" (Berg 1968). Jesus was cast as the true revolutionary of all time and the Bible as the handbook for spiritual revolution, and revolutionary language was subsequently integrated into the movement's writings (Cowan & Bromley 2008: 123). Berg effectively capitalized on the antiestablishment message that resonated among the alienated hippie youth he sought to influence with the Gospel message, whom he referred to as the "lost generation," reminiscent of H. Richard Niebuhr's descriptions of the "religion of the disinherited" of other revivalist periods (Niebuhr 1929: 30–33; Berg 1973b).

While a degree of diversity and fragmentation has been identified among the revivalist movements loosely classified as the Jesus People Movement, the many commonalities these shared are readily identifiable in the COG (Hunt 2008: 1–2). The COG's early beginnings as a coffee shop ministry, and its beach baptisms, street evangelism, and emphasis on the Holy Spirit, prophecy, and the proclamation of an imminent biblical apocalypse were common characteristics of the Jesus People (MacDonald & Stetzer 2020). The belief in a soon-to-unfold fulfilment of the biblical apocalypse, core to the COG's belief system, proved attractive to the counterculture youth of the day in that it "layered neatly upon the counterculture's pervading pessimism about society" (MacDonald & Stetzer 2020). The emotionalism and experientialism of the Jesus People were likewise central to the COG (Richardson & Davis 1983: 400–1), as well as a "Jesus-centric" approach and focus on love (Drakeford 1972: 34–36; Ellwood 1973: 81). The Jesus People's "fundamentalistic insistence on the simple gospel," and an "essentially anti-intellectual, anti-historical, and anti-cultural view of the world" were woven throughout Berg's writings (Enroth et al. 1972: 16). These cultural and theological Jesus People roots served as foundational underpinnings of the religious world of the COG, which would remain constants throughout its history until the Reboot in 2010. The COG's suspicion and rejection of political and educational institutions, materialistic capitalism, secular employment, and institutional Christianity were likewise important to the movement's worldview formation and identity as a "world-rejecting movement" (Wallis 1984: 20–23).

By 1971, a division had arisen between the COG and the Jesus People, due in part to the Children's tendency to proselytize at evangelical universities, which gave rise to accusations of "sheep-stealing" (Eskridge 2013: 184–86). Berg's animosity toward institutional Christianity was extended to the Jesus People, which he dismissed as a superficial movement that had not "dropped out" of the System and would not have a lasting impact (Berg 1971b). In 1972, however, Berg reversed this position and announced that the previously anathematized Jesus People should be cultivated and welcomed, and doctrinal arguments avoided (Berg 1972b; Wallis 1979: 60). Drawn by the COG's high-commitment model and organizational stability, several Jesus People groups joined the movement in

1972, notably Linda Meissner's Jesus Army and David Hoyt's House of Judah and his network of Jesus People houses (Van Zandt 1991: 39; Trott 1995). Hoyt's membership would be short-lived; he departed in 1972 after acrimonious exchanges with Berg (Eskridge 2013: 186–99). Little information is available regarding Meissner's departure from the COG and return to the United States. Her social media page states that she started up a "Jesus People Coffee House" in 2012, and in 2016 she features in a YouTube video calling for a Jesus People revival (Meissner 2015, 2016).

The division between the COG and the Jesus People Movement was further cemented by Berg's introduction of heretical teachings and exploration of New Age spiritualities. Berg embraced astrology in his early writings and envisioned himself as the "water bearer" for the Age of Aquarius commissioned to pour forth "strange new truths" (Berg 1971a). He subsequently claimed to channel spirit guides and interact with mythical gods and goddesses, and later briefly expressed some form of belief in reincarnation (Berg 1973d, 1975a, 1977b). Berg's adoption of cultural themes of the hippie movement and New Age spiritualities, coupled with his subjective interpretations of current events in view of an imminent apocalypse, produced a high degree of theological experimentation that served to untether the movement from its fundamentalist Christian roots. Elements of Berg's eclectic borrowing from other religions or spiritualities were visible in the writings of the movement until the Reboot in 2010, at which point all such writings were removed from circulation.

Despite the evolution of the COG in directions that vastly departed from aspects of its evangelical roots, core characteristics that defined the Jesus Movement were paramount throughout its history. The preaching of a simple Gospel focused on salvation, the belief in an imminent apocalypse, communalism, a love-centric message, the use of prophecy, and the emphasis on being Spirit-led remained virtually unaltered. The COG's adherence to its core ideology of reaching the world with the universal Gospel message for the salvation of souls was pivotal to anchoring the membership in a common purpose in the face of constant change and theological innovations (Van Zandt 1995: 127). (For in-depth readings on the COG's early history, see Enroth et al. 1972: 21–54; Davis & Richardson, 1976: 321–39; Wallis 1979: 51–90; Van Zandt 1991: 30–55; Chancellor 2000: 1–33.)

Controversy and Global Dispersion

The Children of God was no stranger to controversy from its earliest days in response to its signature sackcloth vigils and doomsday message of "Woe to America," which engendered much of the early press coverage of the Jesus Movement (Ellwood 1973: 101–9; Eskridge 2013: 66–67). Berg intentionally leveraged controversy in his writings to etch boundaries of separation from denominational Christianity and mainstream society and rationalized that negative publicity and opposition would ultimately serve to disseminate the movement's message and attract new converts (Berg 1985). While this arguably proved to be the case in the movement's early history, opposition and controversy would become a trademark of the COG and eventually threaten its ability to expand and flourish. Members understood that their high-commitment style of biblical discipleship and their antiestablishment worldview would inherently generate controversy, in conjunction with their vocal denunciations of the perceived corruption of secular society and the accommodation of mainstream churches to secularization. In addition, public activism in the form of protests, sit-ins, public prayer vigils, and en masse visits to churches, known as "church invasions," further engendered oppositional responses (Enroth et al. 1972: 30–34). Members were arrested for proselytizing on university campuses and for public demonstrations, garnering front-page headlines; the group was the subject of criticism from mainstream churches, parents of members, and sensationalistic journalism alike (Van Zandt 1995: 131).

The negative publicity and growing opposition the early Teens for Christ experienced, in conjunction with prophecies proclaimed by some members that

Figure 1 An early street demonstration of the Children of God, highlighting their call to a "revolution for Jesus." Photo courtesy of the Family International.

California would suffer an earthquake and sink into the Pacific, led the small group to relocate to Tucson in a move called "the Exodus" (Van Zandt 1991: 34). Members subsequently traveled in small teams throughout the United States and eventually seventy-five members gathered in Laurentide, Canada. By that time, Berg had come to the realization that a formal organizational model was needed, which he introduced in 1970 by establishing communal households – referred to as colonies, and later homes – as the foundation for the group's organizational structure (Berg 1970a). During their stay at Laurentide, Berg adopted the name Moses David, or Mo, which per his account was received in prophecy by some of the followers, and his writings subsequently became known as "Mo Letters" (Berg 1972c). Prophecies received by the followers in this early period were occasionally published and considered prophetic direction, a practice largely abandoned once Berg fully asserted his prophetic authority.

After departing from Laurentide, the Children reassembled in Washington, DC, dressed in sackcloth and ashes, wearing yokes and bearing staves, for a public vigil to mourn the death of Senator Everett Dirksen, who was an advocate for Bible reading in public schools (Wallis 1979: 56). From there, the Children traveled to Philadelphia, and subsequently to Times Square and the UN building in New York City, to symbolically mourn the death of freedom and the prophesied impending demise of the nation. This doomsday message of the fall of America would be a continuous thread throughout Berg's writings and prophetic predictions. It was during this period of public protest that the group was dubbed the Children of God by a local reporter in New Jersey, who found them camped in a junkyard behind a truck stop (Berg 1972c).

Following these travels, Berg leveraged his relationship with Fred Jordan to assemble a colony on Jordan's property, the Texas Soul Clinic (TSC), as well as a second colony on skid row in Los Angeles. The Texas commune adopted a self-supporting model whereby members could be largely independent from society and attract followers through their exuberant example of Christian discipleship. The TSC colony was the subject of an NBC *First Tuesday* two-hour documentary, "The Ultimate Trip," which aired in 1971. The nationwide coverage this documentary generated resulted in a significant influx of new members to the COG, as well as national attention to the Jesus Movement (Eskridge 2013: 129, 180). By March 1971, one year after settling at TSC, the COG's ranks had grown to more than 500 full-time disciples. The TSC experiment was short-lived, however, as the group had a falling out with Jordan that same year, at which time he evicted them from his properties.

The fledgling movement expanded rapidly throughout the United States and Canada from 1969 to 1972, and as it grew in numbers, countermovement opposition likewise intensified. A group of concerned parents whose children had dropped out of university or left home to join the COG coalesced in San Diego in 1972 to form FREECOG (Free the Children of God), which has been identified as the first anticult movement (Shupe & Bromley 1994: 5–8). Parents accused the movement of kidnapping, hypnotizing, and brainwashing members, and advocated for government intervention. As opposition to the movement mounted, Berg departed from the United States in December 1970 with his wife and ultimate successor, Karen Zerby (known in the movement as Maria Fontaine), first to Israel and subsequently to Europe (Van Zandt 1991: 37–38). This early opposition would have a profound effect on the movement's organizational development and identity as a persecuted church. The theme of persecution on the grounds of religious belief became integrally woven into the writings, music, ideology, and expectations of members as the biblically ordained outcome of their Christian testimony and a precursor to the impending period of apocalyptic tribulation.

While in Europe, Berg announced his retirement from public life and went into seclusion; the vast majority of the approximately 35,000 people who joined the movement at some point in its history would never meet Berg (or Maria) in person. From 1971 onward, Berg directed the movement solely through the published Mo Letters, which he rationalized would provide uniform guidance to the rapidly expanding movement (Berg 1970c). After Berg's relocation, he published a revelation that the descent of the United States into chaos was imminent and consequently members needed to "escape" to other lands in a "massive exodus of the Children of God from North America" (Berg 1972e). This expansion outside of North America, initially to Western Europe, Latin America, and Asia, produced vigorous growth and innovation – by 1973, the membership had expanded to 2,200 members in forty countries on six continents (Van Zandt 1991: 43). It did not, however, usher in a surcease from the controversy that surrounded the movement, as will be further explored in Section 3.

Organization and Reorganization

The longevity and global expansion of the Children of God in comparison to other Jesus People groups has been attributed in large part to the movement's organizational stability (Enroth et al. 1972: 22). Berg developed a leadership hierarchy in 1970, featuring himself as the movement's leader and prophet presiding over a framework of ordained leaders on international, national, and regional levels, which would remain in place in various iterations for most of the movement's history. After Berg's retirement into seclusion, he exercised his

Figure 2 Children of God performing street evangelism in Hyde Park, London, 1972. Photo courtesy of the Family International.

authority primarily through his writings and appointed leadership, who were charged with the oversight of the communes and implementation of the organizational initiatives introduced in his writings. In 1975, Berg formalized the movement's upper-end administrative infrastructure, known as World Services (WS), initially as a communications center "to merely collect, analyze and disseminate information" regarding worldwide operations and the COG's constituency (Berg 1975b). However, as the membership grew from 4,598 members in 1975 to nearly 10,000 members (including children) by 1985, WS continuously expanded its services and authority. Its operations were cloaked in secrecy, and information regarding locations of its residences, known as units, and personnel were safeguarded from the membership and public alike, which Berg rationalized as imperative to the protection of his personal security as a "fugitive in exile, a religious refugee in hiding" (Berg 1970b). Heightened government scrutiny and alarmist media coverage of new religions in the aftermath of the Jonestown mass murder–suicides in 1978 further intensified the COG's separation from and suspicion of the System, deepening the divide between its internal religious world and public persona, as well as reinforcing boundaries of separation between WS and rank-and-file members.

Throughout its history, the movement's organizational structure experienced periodic pendulum swings between cycles of intrusive leadership and institutional regimentation and shifts to local autonomy and democratized oversight processes (Amsterdam 1995). For example, in an early account of the COG, Enroth and colleagues described the movement as "highly authoritarian" (Enroth et. al 1972: 53), whereas in 1976, Davis and Richardson reported it to be "among the most democratic and non-authoritarian of Jesus movement organizations" with a rational bureaucracy in place (Davis & Richardson 1976: 338–39). In Van Zandt's analysis, the movement's pattern of alterations between "direct charismatic guidance and legal-rational authority" afforded an effective and flexible organizational structure that enabled the movement to adaptively respond to new conditions (Van Zandt 1991: 55). As a rapidly expanding and highly experimental movement, shifts in focus or organizational structure would be introduced on a regular basis in response to evolving internal issues and the societal landscape.

In 1978, in response to complaints of leadership abuses of authority and lack of autonomy of the grassroots membership, Berg unexpectedly announced the abolishment of the leadership structure in a significant reorganization known as the Reorganization Nationalization Revolution (RNR) (Berg 1978b). Berg proclaimed that the RNR represented the ushering in of an era of personal freedom, decentralization, and a minimalist organizational framework, with focus on nationalizing local leadership (Berg 1978b). A size limitation was imposed on the communes, which had gradually grown in numbers to an average of more than 100 people, resulting in excessive bureaucracy and regimentation, a recurrent trend throughout the movement's history. The name Children of God was abandoned at this time and initially "the Family of Love" was adopted and later shortened to "the Family." In 1981, in response to the subsequent fracturing of movement cohesion post-RNR, Berg introduced the "Fellowship Revolution" to recreate community and to institute a democratic process for electing local leaders (Berg 1981b).

By the early 1990s, as Berg aged and Maria sought to institutionalize child-rearing practices to accommodate the needs of the children and their socialization, the leadership's mandate once again gravitated toward the institutionalization of norms and restrictive oversight of the homes. Berg's death in 1994 did not produce any notable upheaval, largely due to his earlier affirmations of Maria and her divine appointment as his successor (Berg 1978c). Maria had in any case already assumed leadership of the Family in practice, while Berg had largely relinquished his role in administrative affairs. Steve Kelly – known as Peter Amsterdam within the movement and a visible leadership figure from the late 1980s onward who represented Berg and Maria to the Family at large – became codirector of the movement in 1995, an appointment attributed to Berg's posthumous wishes expressed in prophetic messages (Fontaine 1995b). Under Peter's direction, significant steps were undertaken to democratize the movement's organizational structure, foster personal autonomy, and decentralize the communal homes, which once again had burgeoned in size. To this end, Peter initiated a collaborative process to develop a charter of members' rights and responsibilities, a statutory document that would serve to codify the movement's beliefs, practices, membership requirements, and regulations (The Family International 2020). The Family's Charter represented a novel legal–rational response to internal pressures emergent with the coming of age of the second generation and their demands for change and external pressures in the aftermath of the government raids and court cases of the early 1990s (Shepherd & Shepherd 2007b: 235–36).

Prior to publication of the Charter in 1995, an extensive analysis of the state of the movement was conducted, which included workshops with rank and file members to garner their perspectives regarding the need to modernize the movement's organizational structure, community norms, and membership requirements. The initial draft of the Charter was reviewed by more than 200 members, many of whom were second-generationers, and a final vote was conducted at a continental leadership meeting (Shepherd & Shepherd 2005: 72). The first edition of the Charter was a lengthy document exceeding 300 pages that comprehensively outlined members' rights and responsibilities and codified in great detail its methods of government and membership requirements. The autonomy and democratization of the communal homes introduced by the Charter was instrumental in bringing resolution to troublesome areas, enabling members to adaptively respond to changes in their local sociocultural contexts, while limiting leadership's authority and intervention in the homes. The new size limitations for the communal homes resulted in rapid expansion, as members set up missions in new countries and embarked on innovative outreach initiatives and social gospel ministries. Less than a year after the implementation of the Charter, an increase of 117 percent was recorded in the number of Family homes, which rose from 230 to 499 homes (Fontaine 1995d). The Charter process accorded a participative role to the second generation and served as the impetus for the ensuing integration of second-generation members into leadership and World Services. The Charter was amended and updated in 1998, 2003, and 2009 as new issues emerged and were addressed, which resulted in further layers of organizational requirements and regulations being added. While the original Charter bestowed greater autonomy to the membership and homes, due to the periodic addition of new regulatory measures to address emergent issues, over time it served to regiment the homes and limit members' ability to exercise self-determination (Amsterdam 2010a).

The democratization process modeled by the Charter was enhanced by the establishment of a board structure in 2002 that provided a venue for membership participation in the movement's direction at the local, regional, and national levels. Staffed by up to 500 members worldwide, the boards represented a concerted effort to foster grassroots participation in decision-making and management, and proved to be a catalyst for modernization in numerous spheres of Family life (Shepherd & Shepherd 2005: 77–78). However, as has typified organizational shifts in the movement, aspects of the board structure gradually shifted to a top-down hierarchy, as the international board chairpersons, who were resident members of World Services under the supervision of Maria and Peter, became the authoritative voice in board matters and decisions beyond the local level. The board structure nonetheless proved effective in modernizing diverse pillars of Family life and providing emphasis on programs for children and youth, as well as serving as a mechanism for membership participation in the movement's direction and implementation of initiatives.

Throughout the various iterations of TFI's organizational structure, World Services endured as the top-level leadership body. After Berg's death, his security protocols of secrecy and reclusiveness were retained for WS units, deemed expedient due to TFI's history of conflict with anticult organizations, detractors, and law enforcement (Shepherd & Shepherd 2009b: 10). Members of WS were charged with the production of TFI's publications and the oversight of leadership on the field, and in that capacity were exempted from many requirements of the membership. Perhaps inevitably, WS evolved to some extent into a subculture within a subculture, given its distinct status and separateness from the Family homes and the difficulties and financial struggles of the movement at large. The communes faced sizeable challenges in raising and homeschooling large numbers of children due to birth control prohibitions; fundraising for financial support in developing nations; conducting Christian outreach and humanitarian work; and dealing with external opposition and negative media. In contrast, WS homes generally had few children, were financially supported by members' tithes, exempted from participation in public outreach and evangelism, and shielded from public scrutiny.

As the second generation came of age, open questioning began to circulate regarding WS, resulting in responses from Maria and Peter, such as "The Way Things *Really* Are in WS," which sought to address claims that WS was "out of touch" and "removed from frontline field life" (Fontaine & Amsterdam 2000). Notwithstanding these critiques of WS in the early 2000s, in retrospect the administrative body was central to TFI's establishment as a stable transnational religious community. On an international scale, WS provided numerous services, including administration and inhouse publishing centers; the disbursement of tithes to subsidize services and aid to mission centers; coordination of translations of its publications into numerous languages; and the sponsorship of programs for the care and education of children. World Services was officially disbanded at the Reboot in 2010 and replaced by TFI Services, an abbreviated administrative framework of independent contractors charged with providing limited membership services.

Deconstruction and Revisionism: The Reboot

By the early 2000s, the implementation of the Charter and the board structure with representative grassroots involvement had introduced strides toward democratization, modernization, and accommodation to the needs of the upcoming generations (Shepherd & Shepherd 2009b: 30–32). Second-generation members had been integrated into every layer of leadership, and a methodical approach toward church growth strategies and financial stability had been introduced, seemingly positioning the movement for membership expansion and movement stability. Paradoxically, the process of modernizing the Family's approach for evangelistic purposes and second-generation retention gave rise to tension between accommodative measures introduced to enhance world-engagement, requiring a lessening of "them" and "us" boundaries, and concerns for the preservation of the movement's radical belief system and culture. From 1998 to 2006, the leadership vacillated between modernization and democratization initiatives and increased leadership intervention and regimentation of the homes through retrenchment campaigns to maintain movement purity. In 2006, Peter announced that leadership's focus would shift from internal issues to congregation-building and missional success by 2008, and in 2009 he announced that this process would necessitate significant change to TFI's organizational structure and culture (Amsterdam 2006, 2009b).

In 2010, after a two-year process of critical examination of every aspect of the movement, the most comprehensive reorganization to date was introduced, christened the Reboot to reflect the magnitude of change this represented. The scope of revisionist change encapsulated in the Reboot was rationalized as necessary for the development of a socially relevant culture conducive to the movement's evangelistic mission and congregation-building objectives (Borowik 2013: 19). Previous membership requirements were rescinded, the former leadership and organizational structure was virtually dismantled, a minimalist model of membership was introduced, and the communal household society model was abandoned (Amsterdam 2010c). The extent of revisionism implemented at the Reboot represented a profound reinterpretation of the movement's previous conceptualizations of Christian discipleship and communal way of life.

The dissolution of the communal household model and the Family's organizational structure resulted in an unforeseen period of upheaval, as many members returned to their home countries after decades of living in foreign lands (Borowik 2018: 66). A new organizational framework was expected to be introduced shortly after the Reboot to foster community among the dispersed membership, but this did not occur as anticipated. After forty-two years of operating as a cohesive communitarian movement with a transnational structure, the movement unexpectedly evolved into an amorphous online networked community. In 2022, twelve years after the Reboot, the lack of a community framework has given rise to challenges in membership retention, the preservation of a shared identity, and fostering movement vitality, as will be explored in Section 5.

2 Beliefs, Culture, and Worldview

Paden's characterization of new religious movements as socially constructed and self-contained universes that create alternative forms of community provides a useful typology for analysis of the Children of God's belief system, culture, and worldview (Paden 1994: 62–63). In an early treatment of the COG, Ellwood observed: "There is no way the Children of God can be evaluated except on religious grounds. ... It is an apocalyptic community of 'dropouts,' motivated by a vision beyond the structures of this ordinary world" (Ellwood 1973: 111). The movement's ideology and doctrine were constructed from its early days on total commitment, separation from the world, and the creation of a countercultural utopian Christian society with evangelism as its core purpose. While the movement retained core fundamentalist evangelical beliefs throughout its history, Berg's writings (and later Maria's) ventured outside doctrinal orthodoxy to embrace theological experimentation, extrabiblical revelation, and heterodox religious practices.

The Family International's belief system and lifestyle were constructed through two primary sources: the leadership's writings (the Letters) and the lived experiences and mission work of grassroots members within the communal homes. The missives issued by the leadership served to establish the shared belief system and worldview, while the grassroots membership was central to the social construction of TFI's culture and community dynamics as these were lived within the homes and situationally adapted to members' local context and social climate. The movement created and sustained a unique and vibrant culture despite the dispersal of its membership in numerous countries and its lack of visible administrative centers or direct contact of its members with upper-level leadership (Bainbridge 2002: 29). This section explores the Family's beliefs, worldview and communalist culture, and the role of revelation and prophecy in the development of the movement's unconventional doctrines and practice.

Beliefs

The Children of God's early belief system was centered in biblical literalism, the conviction that followers were living in the "time of the end," and the consequent urgency of sharing the Gospel with the unsaved. Members memorized Scripture extensively, conducted street evangelism, and composed contemporary 1960s-style music to convey their message. As was typical of the Jesus People, the early disciples distributed evangelistic publications with alternative art styles and comics and a message that resonated with countercultural youth. The movement was founded on core fundamentalist evangelical doctrines, which were maintained throughout the movement's history, notably salvation by faith in Jesus, eternal life for the believers, the resurrection and deity of Christ, and Jesus' Second Coming (Melton 1997: 54–55). By the early 1970s, however, Berg's writings and teachings became increasingly untethered from Christian orthodoxy, which gave rise to concerns among evangelical leaders of heretical teachings likewise taking root in the Jesus People and the determination to ensure the movement was rooted in orthodox theology (Eskridge 2013: 206–8).

Christian discipleship with the COG modeled Niebuhr's "Christ against culture" paradigm with its requirements of separation from the world, renunciation of secular and materialistic pursuits and relinquishment of earthly goods to the movement, referred to as "dropping out" and "forsaking all" (Niebuhr 1951: 47–49). The forsaking of earthly possessions and commitments was grounded in a literalist interpretation of Jesus' statement recorded in the Bible: "So likewise, whoever of you does not forsake all that he has cannot be My disciple" (Luke 14:33 NKJV). The membership requirement of dropping out represented a renunciation of the System as antithetical to true Christian discipleship as per the biblical warning that "friendship with the world is enmity with God" (James 4:4; Berg 1974). Berg viewed most established institutions with suspicion and as agents of an ungodly world. He consistently challenged the status quo, social conventions, and traditional Christian mores in his writings. Berg's missives placed little focus on social transformation until the early 1990s, at which time he encouraged members to develop charitable and humanitarian works, which subsequently became an integral part of members' missionary work (Berg 1991).

Berg understood that the COG's "Revolution for Jesus" was unlikely to grow, given its radical nature, tension with society and the perceived shortness of time; therefore, leading people to salvation in Christ was of first importance, as opposed to new member recruitment (Berg 1970d). The COG preached a simple, love-focused Gospel message, epitomized by its signature song, "You've Gotta be a Baby to Go to Heaven." During Berg's brief attendance at Bible college, he had become disenchanted with "theological arguments, philosophical hair-splitting and ridiculous folderol" and declared that the "Gospel of God's love" was "so simple that a child can understand" and was the solution to all of humankind's problems (Berg 1981a). A degree of tension between faith and intellectualism is visible in Berg's writings, as well as in Maria's, due to the conceptualization of the mind and intellect (and higher education) as potentially antithetical to faith, belief in the supernatural, and the primacy of love (Berg 1977a, 1980; Fontaine 2002).

Berg declared that his writings were an extension of the Bible, and in practice superseded the Bible as contemporary revelation; however, he also admitted that his writings were fallible and on occasion acknowledged that viewpoints he expressed were flawed (Berg 1988; Van Zandt 1995: 129). His writings were generally drawn from transcriptions of recordings of informal meetings, conversations with Maria, or table-talk sessions addressing a range of issues, from new revelation and doctrine to mundane pragmatic topics and critiques of cultural or political issues. Van Zandt identified five ideological strands in Berg's writings: personal salvation and the duty to bring the salvation message to the unsaved; total commitment to God's work; "utopian-socialistic" criticisms of capitalist society and its institutions; the imminent introduction of the millennium; and an active spirit world populated by spiritual beings and the spirits of deceased figures (Van Zandt 1995: 129–31). Berg's writings tended to be flamboyant, unpolished, and at times repetitive, frequently containing unedited invectives aimed at political figures, perceived problems of members or former members, or challenges to his authority. His positions on issues were inconsistent or self-contradictory in some cases due to the lack of editorial oversight and their extemporaneous nature or Berg's evolving perspectives. When presented with contradictions to previously articulated positions, Berg occasionally expressed bewilderment that members had taken his writings seriously on the issue or had misunderstood his intent (Berg 1992).

The continuous publishing of new revelations and truth claims fostered a climate of novelty and unpredictability, as the "revelation of the day" overwrote or was aggregated to the previous ideology, or ultimately disregarded if it proved irrelevant to members' lives. WS produced a constant stream of publications from the mid-1980s onward, which often translated into new demands on members' time or level of commitment and ultimately had to be filtered through the realities of everyday life within a complex social environment. In view of the volume and scope of the writings – including revelations of supernatural concepts, doctrinal interpretations, heterodox praxis, and Berg's opinions on a range of issues – members were unlikely to read or retain all that was published, much less integrate every aspect into their personal worldview. The immediate demands of the functioning and financing of the homes and their outreach programs were of foremost importance, and as such, members might subjectively embrace or disregard aspects of the writings foreign to their local situations or irrelevant to their everyday lives (Richardson 2021: 15–16). This interpretive process resulted in a notable variety of opinion and individual expression, as indicated by the findings of Bainbridge's survey of 1,025 members based on the General Social Survey, which identified "considerable diversity of opinion, very much like that found in the encompassing society" (Bainbridge 2002: 169).

When the movement began to come under official scrutiny in the early 1990s, it became apparent that a clear articulation of doctrines and practice was necessary to defend the belief system. To this end, a Statement of Faith was drafted in 1992, couched largely in the terminology of Christian orthodoxy, representing the Family's first attempt to identify and define its core theology. There is no indication that Berg participated in the drafting of the Family's Statement of Faith, which excluded much of the extrabiblical revelation and theological speculation articulated in his writings. The initial intent of this statement, as well as other policy statements issued at the time, was to lessen tension and public hostility and rebrand the Family as a mature religious movement with responsible practices. While the Statement of Faith deemphasized heterodox teachings and unconventional praxis, these continued to proliferate in internal publications from 1995 until 2010, reflecting TFI's historic practice of publishing "esoterica" writings with exclusive truth claims restricted to members, and "exoterica" writings for evangelization and public representation (Cowan 2004: 264).

From its inception, the movement was "fervently apocalyptic" in its belief in the imminence of the biblical apocalypse, referred to as the Endtime, and members' special role in ushering in the Second Coming (Hunt 2008: 18–19). The Family's core eschatological beliefs have been largely consistent throughout its history and harmonize for the most part with standard evangelicalism, grounded in the Gospel accounts in Matthew 24 and Luke 21 and the apocalyptic biblical books of Revelation and Daniel. Berg first announced in 1972 his prediction that the final seven years of the Endtime would begin in 1986 in "The 70-years Prophecy of the End," signaling that the Second Coming of Christ would occur in 1993, which he reiterated often in his writings until 1991 (Berg 1972d). Berg published hundreds of writings on the Endtime featuring interpretations of biblical passages, and speculations on current events and political developments through an apocalyptic lens. He also occasionally issued warnings of momentous world events about to unfold, advising members to prepare by storing food and water or by relocating geographically. The Endtime was also highlighted in the Family's evangelistic message to the public. Throughout its history, the movement produced numerous publications, books, posters, songs, and videos to warn the world of the impending apocalypse, and continues to host a website, Countdown to Armageddon (countdown.org), devoted to the topic (see Figure 3).

The movement's worldview was predicated on the belief that the Second Coming would occur within the membership's lifetime, a context that guided organizational, parenting, and missional strategies. In an unprecedented redirection, Peter postulated in 2009 that Endtime events may not occur for fifty years or more. Consequently, he indicated that the movement needed to shift to long-term strategies for church growth and future generations (Amsterdam 2009b). Notwithstanding such efforts to modify TFI's Endtime worldview and deemphasize it in publications, belief in the imminent rise of a one-world government continues to be a significant identity marker and theological cornerstone for many members and former members (Borowik 2018: 71).

Figure 3 The Countdown to Armageddon website hosts original books, articles and artwork featuring TFI's Endtime beliefs. Screen capture published with permission from the Family International.

Prophecy and Revelation

Prophecy and ongoing revelation represent core beliefs that have been preserved throughout TFI's history, affirmed in its Statement of Faith as the belief that God "continues to speak today" and to "impart His message through revelation and prophecy" (The Family International 2010). Prophecy and progressive revelation were central to the charismatic identities of both Berg and Maria, and their prophetic revelations were placed on an equal footing with the Bible (Chancellor 2008: 19). In 1972, Berg proclaimed his role as God's prophet for the latter days, and credited Maria, the daughter of a Pentecostal minister, with his identity transformation, as she had encouraged him to channel prophecy and revelation and to adopt a prophetic calling (Berg 1972c, 1978c; Wallis 1982: 31–32). Berg's subsequent withdrawal into seclusion in 1972 was instrumental to the social construction and maintenance of his charismatic authority and mystique as "the prophet on the mountain" (Davis 1984: 6; Shepherd & Shepherd 2006: 34). Wallis proposed that Berg's charisma was a precarious property that required ongoing reinforcement and restriction of access from those who would discredit his status (Wallis 1982: 38). Berg further reinforced his prophetic role through his periodic publishing of writings censuring leaders or members who had expressed doubts or defied his leadership, thereby underscoring the fact that open questioning or criticism of God's prophet would not be tolerated.

Berg's writings were rarely presented in the form of prophetic utterances, which were infrequent and diminished over time. His doctrinal innovations, biblical interpretations, and organizational revolutions generally were presented as his own expositions in colloquial language, which he claimed as revelation (Shepherd & Shepherd 2006: 34). His writings sought to present new truths that often added to or countermanded traditional theology, resulting in exclusive truth claims based on novel revelation and special knowledge available only to members (Berg 1975a). Berg introduced numerous spiritual themes that resonated with popular interest in supernatural phenomena of the time, including magic, spirit guides, ghosts, UFOs, and the attribution of spiritual power to objects such as pyramids and crystals (Richardson & Davis 1983: 406). After Berg's death, Maria institutionalized the channeling of messages from Jesus and departed people, including Berg, and augmented the focus on magical and supernatural powers and spiritual beings.

Berg made a number of specific prophetic predictions, most significantly the timeframe for the last seven years before the Second Coming (presumably 1986–93), the destruction of America forty days after Comet Kohoutek's appearance in 1973 (see Figure 4), and various economic crashes. After Berg's revelation

Figure 4 Children of God members perform sackcloth vigils
in 1973 to warn America of the prophesied destruction of America
forty days after Comet Kohoutek's appearance. Courtesy of the Family
International.

regarding Comet Kohoutek did not occur as predicted, he adopted a somewhat
cautious approach and tended to couch these as personal and fallible interpretations, as in the case of his prediction that Comet Halley due to return in
1986 would herald the rise of the antichrist (Berg 1973a, 1984c). Notwithstanding
such cautions, Berg urged members in Western countries to move to "mission
fields" (defined as developing and non-Western nations) to escape a soon-to-come
nuclear holocaust, presumably presaged by the Comet Halley (Berg 1984c). World
Services created a poster for public distribution to warn the world, titled "The
Comet Comes," which predicted that Halley's Comet was an annunciation that "the
last seven years of Man's history and reign on Earth is due to begin very soon!"
(World Services 1987).

When the comet failed to usher in the rise of the antichrist, Berg constructed
what Dawson has referred to as "a sufficiently plausible reinterpretation of events"
(Dawson, 1999: 65). Berg proposed that the prophesied events had occurred
"behind the scenes" rather than in the visible, verifiable way expected, an approach
that served to maintain cultural coherence and doctrinal integrity, while avoiding
the appearance of failure (Berg 1986a; Melton 1985: 21). Berg subsequently
tended to embed fail-safes into his prophetic predictions in case the foretold
event did not come to pass, deeming such instances a misinterpretation on his

part or that of members who had misunderstood his intent (Van Zandt 1991: 55). As it became evident that Berg's timeline for the Endtime was not materializing as he had repeatedly affirmed, he speculated in a series titled "What If?" that the rise of the antichrist had been a secret event and the antichrist was already in place behind the scenes (Berg 1986c). This, too, proved to be an unfulfilled prediction, along with earlier prophetic predictions that identified 1993 as the year of the Second Coming of Jesus Christ.

After Berg's death, a novel conceptualization of disconfirmed prophecy was constructed in a publication authored by Maria, titled the "Jonah Phenomenon." This Letter presented an argument derived from the Old Testament account of the prophet Jonah sent to prophesy the forthcoming destruction of Nineveh and God's subsequent determination to forego the judgment due to the people's repentance (Fontaine 1994a). Based on this account, a theological rationalization was constructed that God's sovereign will is fluid and changeable, and thus disconfirmed prophecy could indicate that God had changed his mind due to people's decisions or other intervening factors. Members demonstrated a high degree of resilience in reconceptualizing, accepting, or disregarding disconfirmed or failed prophecy and the rationalizations for these, perhaps because of the prolific nature of prophecy and revelation published in "the constant charismatic quest" for new revelation (Shepherd & Shepherd 2006: 50). As 1993 came and went and Berg passed away in 1994, members were unperturbed by the lack of fulfillment of the prophesied Second Coming, likely due to the momentous battle for the movement's survival pursuant to intrusive government interventions. Members' ability to assimilate or disregard failed prophecy also may be attributed to the cultural coherence of TFI's religious world, which Melton identified as a critical compensator; when faced with dissonance, members could rely upon "the broader context of faith" and "the unfalsifiable beliefs out of which religious thoughtworlds are constructed" (Melton 1985: 20). Hence a member interviewed by Bainbridge interpreted the delay of the Endtime in terms of the Family's salvific mission:

> So the Endtime, the end of the world has not come for me or for you. But the end of the world has come for millions of people who have died in the past twenty-five years, and many of them without the gospel. . . . It's the end of the world for them. Are we wrong because we think that time is so short?
> (Bainbridge 2002: 20)

The transition of prophetic authority from Berg to Maria in 1994 proved to be unproblematic, largely due to Berg's advance preparation for his eventual death in his writings that proclaimed that Maria would be a prophetess and would publish profuse amounts of prophecy (Berg 1978a). Maria, however, did not claim to possess the gift of prophecy and consequently compensated for her inability to fulfill this role by instituting an innovative collaborative process for the social construction of prophecy. To this end, WS members were regularly commissioned to channel prophecies on specific issues, which were subsequently reviewed by a team of editors and approved by Maria for publishing as corporate direction for the membership. Shepherd and Shepherd proposed that Maria's approach of leveraging multiple prophetic channels for the generation of TFI's official writings introduced a process of "routinization and democratization of charisma" (Shepherd & Shepherd 2006: 44). While this participatory approach proved effective and introduced diversity, final authority regarding the publishing of prophecy rested with Maria, who would also provide interpretive commentary on the prophecies published in her Letters. In the case of organizational decisions, a somewhat directed approach to prophecy was adopted to confirm decisions already made by leadership and to legitimize policy and organizational directives.

Writings published by Maria and Peter underwent a rigorous process of scrutiny, revision, and affirmation prior to publishing, unlike Berg's extemporaneous writings, which had proved to be highly problematic. The process for the social construction of prophecy thus served to constrain prophetic charisma to existing group norms while providing a mechanism for collective problem-solving and legitimizing leadership directives (Shepherd & Shepherd 2006: 46–48). Members and the homes were likewise encouraged to adopt prophecy for guidance and decision-making, resulting in the diffusion of prophecy throughout the movement.

As second-generationers came of age and began to depart from the movement in increasing numbers from the mid-1990s onward, corporate direction in the writings became focused primarily on TFI's internal world, the sheltering of youth from corrosive influences, and the preservation of "the spirit of the Revolution for Jesus" (Fontaine 2001). The issuance of directives attributed to "Jesus speaking in prophecy" incrementally shifted the organizational structure from the democratization processes introduced via the Charter and the board structure toward centralized authority. Prophecy channeled from 1995 to 2008 increasingly served as an authoritative voice for the legitimization of corporate direction, demands for heightened levels of commitment to discipleship expectations and TFI's belief system, and separation from the world (Fontaine 2010b). In retrospect, prophecy and revelation, a hallmark of Maria's leadership, resulted in the creation of a unique "culture of prophecy" central to the direction of the movement, the establishment of doctrine and policy, and guidance and decision-making processes within the communal homes (Shepherd & Shepherd 2009a: 740–42).

Sexual Beliefs and Practices

From the early 1970s onward, Berg progressively introduced writings that challenged traditional ethics for sexuality and embraced elements of the sexual revolution of the late 1960s, eventuating in the marginalization of the movement from mainstream Christianity (Berg 1984b). In language echoing that of proponents of the sexual revolution, Berg proposed that sexuality was to be celebrated as a natural function and human need, analogous to eating and sleeping, and not repressed but freely expressed (Isserman & Kazin 2000: 150–51). His attribution of a sacramental nature to sex when performed with love bore similarities to the sexual ethics of segments of the hippie generation (Miller 2011: 33–35).

The theological justification for the movement's antinomian sexual practices was constructed in Berg's Law of Love doctrine, which affirmed that Christians had been liberated from the strictures of the Mosaic Law, including the Ten Commandments and its prohibitions of extramarital sexual relations. Berg contended that heterosexual relations between consenting members, regardless of marital status, were morally acceptable insofar as these were conducted in a loving manner with mutual consent and did not harm anyone (Berg 1984a; Melton 1997: 11–12). While Berg insisted that the Law of Love if properly practiced should hurt no one, the potential harm of extramarital relations to marriages and nuclear families or the difficulties experienced by single mothers were rarely contemplated in the Letters. The introduction of the Law of Love doctrine led to a period of extensive theological exploration of sexual themes and experimentation. This doctrine also served as the justification for "flirty fishing" (FFing) a controversial form of evangelistic outreach initiated in 1977 that encouraged members to share God's love by dating and interacting sexually with outsiders as a means of leading them to salvation (Wallis 1979: 78–80; Van Zandt 1991: 46–48; Barker 2016: 408–9). Although the practice of flirty fishing was short-lived (1977–87) and never reinstated after its abandonment, it engendered sensationalistic media coverage that has lingered to the present.

Berg's most polemical statements and theological speculations regarding sexuality were published from 1978 to 1985, wherein he challenged traditional moral boundaries for sexual interaction, including those relating to minors. Berg's promotion of liberal sexual practices with few boundaries or safeguards resulted in incidences of sexual interaction between adults and minors and exposure of children to harm (Fontaine & Amsterdam 2008; Barker 2022: 17–18). In 1986, after complaints of sexual misconduct were reported by several teenagers at a teen gathering in Mexico, child protective measures were introduced prohibiting sexual contact between adults and minors.

These measures were further developed in 1989 with the implementation of an excommunication policy for offenders, followed in 1992 by the issuance of a policy statement from WS strongly denouncing child abuse and exploitation and officially disavowing previously published literature at variance with this position (Borowik 2022: 214–15). The Family's Child Protection Policy was ratified in 1995 in the Charter and the current version of the policy stresses that members are subject to the law regarding reporting crimes of child abuse to local authorities (Barker 2022: 22–23). From 1989 to 1994, WS conducted a "pubs purge," whereby the movement's entire body of literature was systematically reviewed to permanently expunge any writings, theological speculation, or artwork in contravention of these policies (Melton 1997: 55).

Berg's polemical writings on sexuality and the sexual "sharing" practices he promulgated in his writings positioned the movement in high tension with society, culminating in the government raids and court cases of the early 1990s and much of the controversy and stigmatization associated with the movement today (Borowik 2022: 214–15). In 1995, in compliance with a court stipulation for a wardship case in England, Peter and Maria published official acknowledgements that David Berg and his teachings were responsible for cases of children having been subjected to sexually inappropriate behavior and harm prior to the institution of child protection policies (Fontaine 1995a; Barker 2022: 23–24). The intervening magistrate, Lord Justice Ward, emitted a lengthy ruling after three years of intensive investigation, in which he leveled harsh criticisms of past eras of the Family's history, while acknowledging that the movement had undergone reformative changes. Lord Justice Ward concluded that he was satisfied that "the wrongs of the past had been stamped out" and the movement provided a safe environment for children raised within the group (Bradney 1999: 217–18; Borowik 2014: 5–7). In 2007, a series of internal documents titled "The Family's History, Policies, and Beliefs Regarding Sex" was published, which provided a detailed analysis of TFI's sexual history and frank acknowledgments of past errors in Berg's misapplication of the Law of Love doctrine (Amsterdam 2007). The series closed with a public apology to second-generation current and former members who had experienced harm or inappropriate adult/minor sexual contact prior to the institution of child protection policies by the late 1980s (Fontaine & Amsterdam 2008).

By the early 1990s, the movement had approached a relatively more conventional view regarding sexuality, and references to sex were less visible in Berg's writings from 1990 to his death in 1994 (Melton 1997: 11). Shortly after Berg's passing, however, Maria revived a focus on sexual sharing practices in her writings due in large part to concerns of preserving Berg's legacy (Fontaine 1994b). In 1995, a seven-part series titled "The Loving Jesus Revelation" was published, which attributed sexual practices to biblical bride of Christ metaphors, utilizing graphic depictions and erotic language (Fontaine 1995c). This series was followed in 1998 by a twelve-part series designed to revitalize the practice of sexual sharing given its decline in the homes, which Maria attributed to a growing sexual conservatism in the aftermath of the government interventions of the early 1990s (Fontaine 1998). By 2006, references to sexuality were infrequent in the writings as the leadership's focus shifted to membership expansion via noncommunal congregational-style members. In 2010, in preparation for the Reboot, previous doctrines and practices were reviewed to determine whether these were conducive to contemporary evangelistic objectives of reaching the world with a relevant Gospel message. Antinomian sexual practices were significantly deemphasized and writings affirmative of previous beliefs concerning sexuality were removed from circulation (Fontaine 2010a). (For in-depth analyses of the Family's sexual beliefs and practices, see Wallis 1979: 74–90; Melton 1997: 11–26; Chancellor 2000: 94–150; Bainbridge 2002: 117–39; Barker 2022.)

Communal Culture

Communalism was central to the social construction of TFI's belief system and worldview as a world-rejecting, apocalyptical missionary organization, and its "socially-maintained and sacredly-defined cultural milieu" (Smith 1998: 68). The communal homes were pivotal to fostering TFI's collective identity and worldview, serving as "sheltered enclaves" where members were relatively insulated and set apart from the encroachment of external influences (Smith 1998: 67–69). Communal households fulfilled various institutional roles as the members' place of worship, community and residence, and missionary bases for evangelism and charitable works. Children were generally sheltered and schooled at home or in city-wide communal schools, and exposure to the outside world was conducted in supervised environments. Members shared their lives within the structured communal setting that guided most aspects of their daily lives and missional activities, and provided a strong sense of community, belonging, and purpose.

From its inception, the movement was organized as a highly regimented religious society, often conceptualized with army metaphors, and guided by a common vision and coherent set of theological commitments (Chancellor 2008: 19). Berg declared the Children of God a "new society, new culture, and new nation" (Berg 1970a), mirroring Paden's conceptualization of religious movements as communities that collectively construct and occupy their own universe structured around sacred things (Paden 1994: 51–54).

While the COG created an alternative society separate from the surrounding sociocultural environment, the movement nonetheless was economically dependent on it for its primary sources of income in the form of monetary donations and the collection of surplus food and goods (Bainbridge 2020: 163). Although Berg's writings extolled the movement's communal model, he cautioned that communal living represented a "means to an end" to achieve its evangelistic mandate and could be dispensed with if it no longer served this purpose (Berg 1971c). However, the reality on the ground was that the communal lifestyle and shared experiences of the members were essential to the Family's existence and evolution over four decades. A high degree of camaraderie existed among the membership, which outlived the disassembling of the communal homes after the Reboot in 2010 (Borowik 2018: 62–63). Shepherd and Shepherd's visitation of twenty-two communal homes in sixteen countries indicated that members had adapted well to local customs, languages, and evolving conditions in foreign nations, while maintaining the Family's lifestyle, common vision, and theological commitments within the communes (Shepherd & Shepherd 2007a: 42).

Theologically, two foundational principles underpinned the Family's communal society model. First, Berg contended that communalism, as modeled by the early church, was intended to serve as the biblical archetype for believers and required that "all who believed" reside in shared households and have "all things in common" (Acts 2:44). Second, the "One Wife" doctrine, a revelation grounded in biblical metaphors of Christians as the collective bride of Christ, proposed that members were part of a greater marriage and one family – hence the integration of "the Family" into the movement's name from 1979 onward. To develop a cooperative society grounded in these theological principles, members subordinated individual pursuits in favor of community imperatives, worked collaboratively, and shared material and intellectual resources, relinquishing claims to private ownership other than minimal personal possessions. With few exceptions, members of communal homes lived under the same roof or in two or more adjoining properties, which were generally rented in keeping with the nomadic and antimaterialistic nature of the movement. In the aftermath of the movement's "baby boom" of the late 1970s to late 1980s, the ratio of children to adults increased significantly, necessitating a shift in focus to the discipling and socialization of children into TFI's worldview. Berg predicted that the second generation would be "the most revolutionary disciples" given their upbringing in a countercultural Christian utopian lifestyle, where they would grow up "never knowing what 'churchianity' [conventional Christianity] and system jobs and education are like" (Berg 1973c).

The One Wife greater marriage ideology espoused the deemphasis of marriage and the family unit in favor of the interests of the commune and the movement. Children were considered a shared communal responsibility and generalized norms for their upbringing were instituted. Berg's early writings criticized traditional marriage, deeming nuclear families to be "the basis of the selfish capitalistic private enterprise system," and proclaimed that "marriage to God and your relationship with the rest of God's Wife – the Body" should take precedence (Berg 1972a). While Berg periodically acknowledged the importance of marriage and nuclear families, the One Wife doctrine's prioritization of the larger Family remained central to the movement's communal culture and collectivist ideology. In retrospect, the One Wife revelation, coupled with the Law of Love doctrine that normalized sexual sharing within marriages, resulted in disruption of marriages, lack of protections for the family unit, and destabilizing situations for children that produced "permanent organizational scars" (Shepherd & Shepherd 2013: 77). In the early 1990s, as the movement came under official scrutiny, increased focus was placed on nuclear families, and protections and rights for families and children were institutionalized in the Charter in 1995. In 2008, Maria and Peter acknowledged that marriages and families had not been sufficiently safeguarded and issued an official apology, which was reiterated at the Reboot (Fontaine 2010a).

At the Reboot, the Family's historic communal society model was abruptly disassembled, resulting in unprecedented cultural fragmentation, indicative of the critical role of the communal homes in the movement's cohesion and resilience. The shared community and identity members experienced within the homes, notwithstanding the difficulties of communal living, produced an alternative lifestyle and unified subculture that endured for four decades. In Chancellor's analysis of the Family's history and communal culture, he noted that the Family had demonstrated a "remarkable ability to survive repression, persecution, and radical theological shifts" while retaining "a surpassing level of coherence and mutual commitment while spread across the globe" (Chancellor 2000: 250).

3 Media, Court Cases, and Countermovements

The emergence of countercultural religious movements in the 1960s and 1970s that predicated alternative lifestyles and values, defied the status quo, and operated outside the mainstream, gave rise to a range of public responses – from guarded tolerance to consternation, to reprobation and official scrutiny. From its early antiestablishment denunciation of the socioeconomic and religious mainstream to its organization as an alternative new religious movement, the Children of God's history has been characterized by controversy and opposition, punctuated by periods of intensive media scrutiny and extreme cases of government intervention. Berg's introduction of controversial sexual practices in the late 1970s became the predominant focus of media coverage and anticult narratives of the movement, which has endured long after the domestication of these practices from the early 1990s onward and the implementation of child protection policies (Melton 1997: 26–27; Richardson 1999: 177–78). Controversy and opposition variously served as drivers for innovation, accommodation, and retrenchment from the movement's early days of recruitment among the counterculture youth of California to its struggles at the turn of the twenty-first century with adversarial websites and cyber media.

FREECOG, the first cult-watching organization formulated in the United States, emerged in response to the COG's early recruitment efforts and served as the prototype for subsequent anticult organizations (Shupe & Bromley 1994: 5–6; Wright & Palmer 2016: 13–14). This coalition of concerned parents was successful in their lobbying efforts to galvanize politicians, government agencies, and journalists to action, culminating in a critical report on the COG published by the New York Attorney General in 1974 (Wallenstein 1974). The report proved ineffectual, however, since members had largely abandoned the United States in response to the increasingly hostile climate they encountered. In 1979, in light of the social milieu of intolerance that emerged after the Jonestown murder–suicides, Berg issued a call for members to go "underground" to avoid religious persecution and the "moral panic" produced by this event (Introvigne 2000: 48). His writings called for a shift from high-profile evangelistic activities to discreet and less visible methods, such as door-to-door witnessing as modeled by the Jehovah's Witnesses (Berg 1979). Members were exhorted to abandon vestiges of hippie attire and customs, and to assume conventional roles as mature Christian families (Berg 1982). Endeavors to tone down radical elements of the movement's public presentation after Jonestown to avoid scrutiny concomitantly served to entrench the boundaries of separation between the movement and society at large. Whereas previously members had been visible in the public square with their signature musical performances, skits, and unconventional literature, they sought to blend in, while preserving their radical beliefs and practices within the boundaries of their internal world. From this point onward, the movement would continuously grapple with the dialectical tension of fostering a relatively conventional public presence to avoid opposition, attract donors and recruit converts while preserving the Family's "otherness" and radical form of Christianity (Barker 2005: 69–70). Economic imperatives would play a significant role in this tension at the grassroots level, as the homes experimented with various forms of fundraising and adapted situationally to what worked to engage donors, garner financial support, and foster good relations with the public (Richardson 1982: 255–58).

In the aftermath of the tragic events of Jonestown, numerous attempts were enacted by governments to exercise social control over new religions, indiscriminately lumped together as dangerous cults, the most extreme of which were government-sanctioned raids and court cases from the late 1980s throughout the 1990s (Barker 1986: 331–32; Wright & Palmer 2016: 2–6; Richardson 2021: 18–19). These interventions were justified largely on the grounds that the minority religion's belief system and lifestyle practices posed a threat to members' children and to the larger society (Richardson 1999: 174–77). The Family International became a frequent target of social control efforts in the form of paramilitary-style government raids and protracted legal battles from the late 1980s to the mid-1990s (Borowik 2014; Wright & Palmer 2016: 73). These government interventions had profound effects on the evolution of the movement, as it fought for the right to practice its religion and homeschool its children while engaging in extensive efforts at reputation management to decrease tension with the surrounding sociocultural environment and attain legitimacy in the religious marketplace.

After surviving the trauma and stigmatizing media generated by the raids and court cases of the 1990s, the movement faced a new form of crisis in the early 2000s. By that time, the religious debate surrounding new religious movements had been translated to the realm of cyberspace, thereby introducing new factors to the cult wars (Borowik 2017: 113). The Family International encountered opposition in online spaces in the form of adversarial websites and detractor forums; counternarratives disseminated in social media, blogs, and books; cyber media purveying derogatory stereotypes and atrocity tales; and the struggle for reputation management in search engine results for the movement that proved intractable. This section provides an overview of the oppositional forces the movement has faced in its efforts since the early 1990s to distance itself from past controversies and reinvent itself as a contemporary alternative Christian movement.

Government Raids and Court Cases

From 1989 to 1993, dozens of Family communal residences on three continents were subjected to internationally publicized paramilitary-style raids in which scores of members were detained and hundreds of children were taken into state custody. Within a four-year period, government raids and investigations were conducted in Argentina (1989 and 1993), Australia (1992), Brazil (1992), France (1992), Peru (1990), Spain (1990), and Venezuela (1992). The magnitude of these government interventions highlights the precarious position of unconventional new religious movements in the face of oppositional forces comprised of former members, relatives, the media, and state actors. Wright and Palmer's study of government raids identified "remarkably consistent" patterns in the raids conducted on Family communities, notwithstanding enormous geographical differences (Wright & Palmer 2016: 73). Although variations exist in how state interventions were conducted, patterns may be traced in the coalitions that incentivized the raids, and the government response and subsequent legal proceedings despite the diversity of national cultures, legal systems, and constitutional definitions for freedom of religion.

From an analysis of court documents and media coverage surrounding these cases, it is evident that the concerted claims-making of anticult organizations and a handful of apostates, coupled with sensationalistic media accounts, were instrumental in mobilizing authorities to take drastic action under the presumption of concern for the children's well-being. The collective pressure brought to bear on government authorities by these convergent claims and atrocity tales led officials to respond disproportionately and exceed the limits of their jurisdiction with paramilitary raids normally reserved for groups presumed to be armed, such as gangs, terrorists, or drug traffickers (Wright & Palmer 2016: 3). Palmer concluded that the overriding aim of government raids on new religious movements appeared to be "to exhibit the state's control over groups perceived as deviant and as constituting a threat to the moral order" (Palmer 2011: 75). Charges leveled against Family members featured a wide range of offences, including prostitution, drug possession, racketeering, kidnapping, child trafficking, child abuse, illegal association, operating illegal schools, fraud, and offending the moral order.

In the cases of the raids conducted in Argentina, Spain, Australia, and France, Family communal residences were subjected to predawn raids that resulted in lengthy court proceedings and social services interventions. In each incident, scores of heavily armed police officers forcibly entered communes, breaking down doors in some cases, with social services on hand to take the children into care and whisk them away to detention centers. The media were alerted in advance of the raids and were present to capture and broadcast images of the events, which were accompanied by lurid headlines denouncing the group as a "sinister cult" culpable of pernicious acts (Borowik 2014: 8–9). In Argentina, the media were permitted to enter the communes during the raids, resulting in the publishing of photos of children being taken from their beds with little regard for the children's privacy or welfare (Nash 1993). Cult experts played a prominent role from the onset of the proceedings and were consulted by examining magistrates and law enforcement officials and interviewed repeatedly by journalists. Although these self-proclaimed experts did not possess first-hand knowledge of the movement, they spoke authoritatively with generalized rhetoric about the danger of cults and brainwashing, which played a significant role in shaping public opinion and dehumanizing members and their children (Borowik 2014: 8–17).

Family members in each instance were detained on nonspecific charges and were not charged as individuals but treated as guilty by association, based solely on generalized claims of former member and anticult activists. A total of more than 500 children were forcibly removed from their homes, in some cases for several months, and taken into custody by child protection agencies, where they were subjected to intrusive medical, psychological, and educational examinations absent the presence of a parent or advocate, in foreign surroundings and a climate of fear. Protracted interrogations and observations of the "rescued" children failed to render evidence to support the government's actions or claims that the children were victims of neglect or abuse. Social welfare authorities nonetheless were determined to have the children placed as wards of the state or to transfer custody to relatives, while officials scrambled to produce corroboratory evidence to rationalize the raids and continued to reassure the public that such evidence existed (Borowik 2014: 11–12; Wright & Palmer 2016: 75). In the final instance, the courts dismissed the charges in each case, returned the children to their parents, and declared that the charges filed were either groundless, false, or unsubstantiated. The rulings of the courts in Spain and Argentina severely criticized the government interventions, comparing these to witch hunts and the Spanish Inquisition (Oubiña et al. 1992; Prack et al. 1993). The courts' decisions were subsequently appealed, and in each case the lower courts' rulings were upheld by the appeals courts and supreme courts in Argentina, Spain, Australia, and France (Borowik 2014: 12–18).

The favorable outcomes of the legal proceedings of Family members in Argentina, Australia, and Spain resulted in significant juridical precedents upholding religious freedom protections (Borowik 2014: 3–4). Nevertheless, media coverage of these events did not accurately reflect the court outcomes in most cases, due to what Wright refers to as the "front-end/back-end disproportionality" problem, whereby equal media space is rarely granted when cases are resolved in favor of new religions (Wright 1997:107–9). This pattern is readily identifiable in the government raids of Family homes in Argentina, where the case was covered daily at the front-end stage of the raids by Western media outlets with unbridled speculation on egregious crimes committed, decrying horrific conditions endured by children of the "sex cult." When the appeals court ruled in favor of the members and excoriated the intervening authorities, deeming them to have conducted "an illegal investigation and arbitrary use of penal power," the story received scant coverage by Western media (Prack et al. 1993; Wright 1997: 108). Concerned Argentine journalists protested the inhumane treatment and human rights abuses experienced by members, while expressing alarm at the government's overreach (Ruiz Nuñez 1993). But such concerns were not raised by Western media even after the appeals court exonerated the members and upheld constitutional guarantees of religious and human rights. The Australian Supreme Court's ruling determining that the raids of Family homes had been unlawfully conducted likewise merited only brief mentions in the Australian news and none in the international press (Dunford 1999).

The fact that the courts exonerated the members and returned all the children to their parents after months of intensive investigation conducted in hostile circumstances, along with the presumption of guilt that fueled these state interventions, offers hope for the future of religious tolerance in the legal forum. Paradoxically, the well-being of children was cited as the rationalization for the extreme measures adopted in the raids conducted, while the courts' findings concluded that the government interventions had placed children at risk (Borowik 2014: 4). The trauma incurred by Family members and their children due to the raids, familial ruptures, threats by authorities, media stigmatization, and inhumane treatment while in custody has rarely been the subject of reflection, as Shepherd and Shepherd noted:

> What was the net result of all these separate investigations following the terrorizing of large numbers of children and adults, mass arrests, imprisonments, custody placements, invasive examinations, and breakup of households? Not a single case against Family adults was upheld in courts of law within the various countries involved. Not one of the more than 600 children examined by doctors and psychologists in these countries was found to have been abused. In every country, in every case, parents and children were released from custody for lack of evidence and eventually reunited. (Shepherd & Shepherd 2011: 238)

The government raids of the 1990s placed the movement at the center of a formidable battle for its survival in the face of government intrusion, discriminatory practices, and hostile media (Richardson 1999: 181). In response, members staged protests around the world, decrying the brutality of the raids, the inhumane treatment of children, and mass incarceration of adults as religious persecution and human rights violations. In the aftermath of the raids, it became evident that strategies for lowering tension and fostering constructive relations with the wider community were in order, as well as adopting greater transparency regarding the movement's beliefs and practices. Official policy statements were issued articulating Family beliefs, practices, and stances on issues that had given rise to controversy, which were subsequently codified in the Charter. Public relations representatives were appointed to proactively engage the media and lobby for religious tolerance, and journalists, academics, and representatives of government agencies were invited to visit Family homes. Family members developed charitable and humanitarian works that benefitted their local communities and served to allay suspicions due to their alternative lifestyle. The Family International's communal culture, unconventional beliefs, and heterodox sexual ethics nonetheless would continue to render the movement vulnerable to claims-making by countermovements, detractors, and the media (Borowik 2014: 5–7). (For in-depth accounts of TFI raids and court cases, see Melton 1997: 34–46; Richardson 1999: 172–86; Bainbridge 2002: 1–20; Palmer 2011: 61–65; Borowik 2014: 3–23; Wright & Palmer 2016: 73–98).

Second-Generation Counternarratives

The shift in demographics to an increasingly second-generation majority by the early 1990s ushered in unavoidable processes of change, as the care, indoctrination, and socialization of children and teenagers became of increasing importance in the homes (Barker 1995a: 165–71). In the early 1980s, Berg declared the first cohort of second-generation children to be adult members of the community by age twelve, referencing Jewish bar mitzvah practices, which resulted in their integration at a young age into community activities and responsibilities, a practice that proved untenable and was subsequently discarded (Amsterdam 2009a). He further proposed that the equivalent of a junior high school education would be sufficient for the second generation, given the education they would obtain in the Bible and Family writings, and expectations of the imminent unfolding of the Endtime (Berg 1975c). The assumption that children would remain in the movement was embedded in the development of educational and child-rearing practices, though clearly that would not be the case, considering that the Family experienced a relatively high turnover rate of its membership throughout its history.

In *Perfect Children,* van Eck Duymaer van Twist observed that the first wave of children born into new religious movements uniquely experiences the tumultuous process of experimentation and adaptation that often occurs as the movement makes adjustments to accommodate a growing second-generation population (van Eck Duymaer van Twist 2015: 7). As the Family's first cohort of children became teenagers and began to question and rebel against community norms, leadership responded by introducing teen programs to promote second-generation engagement in the "Revolution for Jesus" and commitment to the movement's belief system and worldview. In the early 1990s, the Discipleship Training

Revolution, Victor Programs, and Teen Training Centers were launched to socialize teens into Family norms based on high-commitment expectations for Christian discipleship, and to curb behavior and attitudes discordant with Family ideology. These programs, which in some cases utilized excessive disciplinary measures, contributed to the alienation of a significant percentage of the first cohort of second-generationers, and were abandoned by 1994 (Chancellor 2000: 233–45; Barker 2016: 415–17). The Family Discipline Guidelines were introduced in 1994 to codify acceptable disciplinary measures, and subsequent official apologies were issued for previous disciplinary excesses (World Services 1994; Fontaine & Amsterdam 2009a).

Numerous reforms and accommodations were introduced in the Charter in 1995 to address the needs of second-generationers and incorporate them into positions of responsibility. The movement nonetheless continued to struggle in its quest to develop socialization processes conducive to the retention of the second generation without compromising its historic world-rejecting ideology. Concerns about the preservation of TFI's radical roots, coupled with high expectations for second-generationers to adhere to religious and behavioral norms, failed to take into consideration the differences between the "born agains" and "born intos" (Barker 1995a: 168–71). Amid this ongoing tension, a subculture "on the margins" emerged among the youth who possessed a shared cultural identity forged by their experiences growing up in an alternative community, as well as their questioning of social and spiritual reality as understood within the movement (Barker 1998: 87–88).

By the early 2000s, a significant number of second-generationers had departed and began to connect online and network on the Moving On website (defunct since 2009), where resources for their transition to society were posted and space was provided to share experiences and grievances. Concomitantly, a wiki page (xfamily.org) was created with the stated intent of making public TFI's internal publications and archiving countermovement literature, although in Bainbridge's analysis, "the net effect of the site was to discredit the organization" (Bainbridge 2020: 164–65). While Moving On was initially created as a support mechanism to assist second-generationers in the leave-taking process, the discussion forum became increasingly adversarial, with calls for the termination of the movement and its leadership. Family leadership responded in kind to this perceived threat by publishing its own counternarratives, thereby contributing to the polarization of the debate and ratcheting up of hostilities (Fontaine & Amsterdam 2009a). An unofficial pro-TFI website also was launched by second-generation members (myconclusion.org), where more than 400 current and former second-generationers posted their views and countered claims made by Moving On posters.

At the height of this tension, in early 2005 Maria's estranged son, Ricky Rodriguez, murdered former member Angela Smith and subsequently committed suicide after filming a disturbing video, widely reproduced and still accessible on YouTube seventeen years later (Bainbridge 2017: 99–100). This tragic event placed the movement once again at the center of stigmatizing media coverage, effectively canceling public credibility gains from TFI's previous court vindications. In the aftermath of this incident, TFI's leadership sought to promote reconciliation and dialogue with the former second-generation community. Official apologies were published that validated grievances expressed by second-generationers and acknowledged leadership's responsibility for insular practices that had disadvantaged them in their transition to society, while reiterating apologies for past cases of harm and sexual misconduct (Fontaine & Amsterdam 2009a). Rodriguez' actions served to focus attention on the unique issues that second-generationers experience in the process of disaffiliation from a high-commitment communal movement, further problematized by the rupture of familial and community ties. These problems were addressed to some extent for subsequent cohorts as TFI gained greater awareness of its responsibility to assist departing young people. Resources were developed to facilitate the transition process for second-generationers, who also had access to online support networks developed by other second-generationers (van Eck Duymaer van Twist 2015: 186; Amsterdam 2009a).

Interviews with second-generation leave-takers recorded in *Perfect Children* indicated that many had experienced a crisis of identity or "fragmented identity" due to "a sense of discontinuity in the storied selves that make up a narrative identity" (van Eck Duymaer van Twist 2015: 189). The transition to the wider culture could be further problematized in the case of TFI due to the second generation's limited exposure to public schooling, secular employment, and in some cases, their home country or native tongue. Former members of all ages indubitably have faced a challenging task of recreating their identity post-TFI, in view of stigmatizing media aimed at rousing public hostility and denigrating new religions. The disclosure of previous affiliation with a "cult" widely perceived as subversive is problematic, other than as a narrative of victimhood, given the dynamics of contemporary cancel culture leveraged via social and online media as a means of exclusion and exertion of social pressure (Clark 2020: 88–89). Since the early 2000s, escape narratives have become prevalent in public claims-making of former TFI second-generationers, a variation of earlier first-generation captivity narratives grounded in brainwashing, coercion, and subversion claims (Bromley 1998: 5–7). Second-generation escape narratives published in books, films, podcasts, and the media have variously served to express grievances, call for action against the movement, or to gain social capital and name recognition for entrepreneurial purposes such as book sales and business pursuits, indicative of the complexity of such narratives (Wright 1998: 109). Counternarratives published by former TFI second-generationers in the past decade have tended to feature narratives of escape and self-empowerment that resonate with the current cultural moment and its focus on "expressive individualism" (Taylor 2007: 299–300, 473). A review of *Sex Cult Nun* by former second-generationer Faith Jones, now an attorney and business consultant, described the book as "a narrative of triumph that one could escape an egregious cult and create an authentic life" (Greymoor 2021).

In an earlier discussion of the anticult movement (ACM), Barker highlighted its role in creating a "secondary construction of reality" of new religions, reinforced by atrocity tales and promulgated by the media as verified claims (Barker 1995b: 297–98). Introvigne noted that such counternarratives tend to be "simple black-and-white stories with clearly identifiable heroes and villains" and lurid atrocity tales, often designed to evoke moral outrage (Introvigne 2022). The contemporary wave of TFI second-generation counternarratives appears to indicate a new dynamic at work, as their personal stories, disseminated by the media as sensationalist cult stories, seem to have displaced the ACM's previous role in contextualizing the narrative as cult experts. The reliability of the accounts of former members turned anticult activists has been discussed at length in the literature (see Bromley 1998); but the dynamics of second-generation counternarratives, which express different kinds of issues and grievances due to their unique lived experiences and context as "born intos," has received less attention.

Van Eck Duymaer van Twist noted that the identity management work necessary to transition between two very different worlds can give rise to reinterpretations of past events, norms, and beliefs in an unfavorable light, further highlighting the complexities of second-generation counternarratives (van Eck Duymaer van Twist 2015: 239). In the case of TFI, second-generation counternarratives published in the media or in books often focus on experiences, practices, or grievances from its earlier history (late 1970s to late 1980s) unique to the first cohort of second-generationers (Barker 2022: 18). Counternarratives of later cohorts have tended to focus on issues of identity, personal autonomy, and the restrictive nature of communal boundaries or norms, and in some cases claim ownership of experiences unique to the first cohort or incorporate anticult tropes and generalized stereotypes (Barrionuevo 2022; Cresswell 2022). It is difficult to determine to what extent the current wave of public counternarratives may be representative of the experiences and animus of second-generation leave-takers in general, given that the vast majority of TFI's "born intos" – estimated at 15,000 – are invisible in the public narrative. Previous scholarly research has indicated that visible, oppositional former members differ from the majority of invisible leave-takers, whose response ranges more typically from ambivalence to "quiet disenchantment" (Wright 1998: 109). Further research is needed to explore the experiences and narratives of former second-generationers, considering the experiential, cultural and contextual differences between the two generations.

Online Cult Wars

In the days of largely print, television, and radio media, numerous scholars of religion expressed concerns regarding the role the media played in constructing narratives that painted a sinister picture of new religions as intrinsically pathological or harmful (Wright 1997: 101). The media undoubtedly played a significant role in creating the "common stock of cultural knowledge" and social construction of cultic narratives, and the promotion of the anticult paradigm of new religions (Richardson 1995: 156–57; Shupe & Hadden 1995: 178–80). From 1969 to the mid-1990s, the long-term impact of such media was somewhat mitigated due to limited public access to previously published print media or radio and television programs. Sensationalistic stories rapidly disappeared from the public imagination and negative programs re-aired occasionally, if at all. While some efforts were made by the media during the 1990s to incorporate scholarly research and responses from new religious movements in their coverage, the overriding interest of the media has been the exposure of movements "as fraudulent, fantastic, or sensational" and to evoke public outrage (Barker 1995b: 299–300).

The gradual incorporation of media to online spaces from 1995 onward and the development of social media and informal news sources led to the relocation of the cult controversy to the more fluid environment of the Internet. Cyberspace has proved to be a largely unregulated frontier where previous norms for balanced and ethical journalism no longer apply to the same extent, and compelling counternarratives may be widely published and easily disseminated without any attempt at verifying their claims. Media coverage of TFI in the last decade has largely responded to the contemporary "infotainment" news trend with its fusion of information-oriented and entertainment-based media genres (Thussu 2008: 7–9). Controversies and counternarratives dating to the 1980s are often presented as current news occurring in real time while failing to mention the findings of the courts and organizational changes implemented in subsequent decades. Streaming services increasingly feature an array of cult programs, such as a 1994 film, *The Children of God*, featuring former members who became anticult activists, available on demand on Netflix

(Smithson 1994). An ethnographic short film, *Children of God: Lost and Found*, produced by a former second-generationer fifteen years ago is likewise available on demand on various streaming services, indicating the permanence of counternarratives online, which increasingly serve as primary information sources for the public (Thomson 2007).

Van Eck Duymaer van Twist noted that the Internet "gives voice to a large spectrum of views and opinions about religious groups, many of them the views of members or former members" which would appear to indicate that the Internet provides equitable access to both voices (van Eck Duymaer van Twist 2015: 180). However, TFI's history indicates an unequal access to online representation for new religions, as legitimate spaces tend to be restricted to the movement's official websites and its own social media, accessed by limited audiences. Counternarratives, to the contrary, are widely disseminated to the public and reproduced on multiple media websites, blogs, social media, podcast sites, and YouTube. Wikipedia, which purports to be "the largest and most-read reference work in history" (Wikipedia 2022), represents yet another online battleground for defining unpopular religious movements, due to the oligarchic editorial power of a small group of early users who have the power to restrict contributions (Bainbridge 2020: 135). TFI's Wikipedia profile was created by a countercult administrator with editorial authority who refused to negotiate edits or allow the introduction of scholarly research to the profile, despite Wikipedia's purported open collaboration model (Borowik 2017: 113).

The Family International has demonstrated significant resilience in navigating a range of opposition and social control efforts throughout its history, featuring anticult actors, career apostates, hostile media, and intrusive government interventions. Despite challenges to its belief system and communal lifestyle, the movement proved adept at weathering adversity, and adapting and accommodating as needed for its survival and the propagation of its evangelistic message. However, the repositioning of the cult wars in online spaces has given rise to a contentious frontier due to the ease in which counternarratives flourish and the climate of social exclusion and delegitimization that may be fostered (Cowan 2004: 268; Borowik 2017: 113–14). Since 2005, TFI has faced virtually insuperable challenges to its efforts to reinvent itself as a mature religious movement that has addressed past error and excesses, due to stigmatizing media, adversarial social media and websites, and the permanence of counternarratives online.

The singular dynamics of the online cult wars arguably have introduced a new form of social control in that the right of unpopular new religious movements to have a voice in the marketplace of ideas or exercise religious freedom may be largely determined by its critics. The propagation of counter-information, unquestioned and treated as authoritative, can be highly damaging to religious minorities due to its permanence in cyberspace and the lack of equal space for response. Derogatory stereotypes can be promulgated with great ease and little cost, resulting in public censure and exclusion, with the effect of canceling the movement in the public sphere. The impact of legal verdicts that have served to uphold and define the free exercise of religion, as in the case of TFI, may be diminished over time, as cyber activists, former member crusaders, and the infotainment media are able to monopolize the defining narrative of new religions in the court of public opinion. This new dimension of the cult wars portends to have a profound impact on the ability of new religious movements to mature beyond their radical roots and to attain legitimacy in the religious marketplace (Borowik 2014: 19–20).

4 Deconstructing and Rebooting the Movement

Having weathered the storms of controversy and government interventions of the early 1990s and introduced accommodative measures and democratization to its organizational structure from 1995 to 2005, the Family appeared to be well positioned to stabilize internally and expand its outreach programs. In 1995, self-regulating policies were institutionalized in the Charter that introduced transparency, upheld members' rights, and delimited leadership authority, and by the early 2000s a framework for grassroots membership participation in the development of the movement had been implemented via the board structure. Second-generationers had been integrated into leadership and management at every level and were instrumental to the implementation of modernization initiatives and innovation to various aspects of the movement. Maria and Peter's roles had evolved from Berg's "iconic prophetic status" to organizational direction and the publishing of the movement's writings by means of collaborative processes (Shepherd & Shepherd 2009b: 11). In Shepherd and Shepherd's analysis, TFI had emerged as a "relatively successful new religious movement through adroit adaptation" to the challenges it faced over the course of its "controversial career," thereby enhancing its organizational viability and prospects for future success (Shepherd & Shepherd 2005: 67). Despite internal growing pains inherent to the coming of age and departure of second-generationers, TFI had maintained a stable level of committed membership, attracted a growing network of noncommunal members and donors, and the homes had developed extensive charitable and humanitarian projects. In 2002, TFI initiated its flagship outreach magazine, *Activated*, now in its twentieth year, a milestone shift from outreach methods focused primarily on one-time encounters to developing a subscribership base and providing a more conventional Christian message.

The change introduced by 2005 represented significant progress and institutional maturation, but it also served to exacerbate the dialectical tension new religious movements may experience between accommodation in response to internal and/or external contingencies and concerns for the retention of the movement's belief system and unique identity (Shepherd & Shepherd 2005: 68). The Letters published by Maria from 1995 to 2005 were largely focused on internal issues in the quest to root out "worldly" incursions and return to the "radical, revolutionary spirit" that gave birth to the movement, with a call to reject any form of "compromise with the System" and secular ideologies (Fontaine 2001). In 2006, after a decade of intensive internal focus, Peter and Maria announced a realignment of leadership's priorities to TFI's core mission of Christian evangelism via the Offensive, a new initiative that would be launched in February 2008 (Amsterdam 2006). In preparation, practical instruction was published for devising congregation-building strategies and new missional approaches to expand TFI's circle of influence and build financial stability. In retrospect, Peter recontextualized this process as a "change journey" that required the virtual abandonment of legacy "mindsets" and approaches and the adoption of new practices and methods to better relate to people in contemporary society (Amsterdam 2009b).

In anticipation of the shift to a new organizational model to accommodate the envisioned membership expansion of less committed congregational members, a protracted process was undertaken to identify aspects of TFI's religious world incongruent with these objectives. Meetings were convened with regional leaders from around the world, member surveys were conducted, and feedback from hundreds of members was compiled and examined by WS leadership. This critical analysis was prompted in part by the realization that TFI membership had never expanded beyond 10,000 members, including children, throughout its history, or sustained significant numbers of external membership (Fontaine & Amsterdam 2009b). Upon completion of this two-year review process, in 2010 Maria and Peter unexpectedly announced that the movement's organizational model was no longer relevant to its evangelistic objectives and dissolved TFI's organizational framework in the most comprehensive reorganization to date, referred to as the Reboot (Amsterdam 2010c; Borowik 2018: 65–66).

World Services released twenty-two Reboot documents in June 2010 that mapped out the organizational, doctrinal, and cultural change to be adopted at the Reboot. Eight of these documents provided the rationale for the shift, including: "Change Journey Manifesto," which focused on ideological arguments (Amsterdam 2010c); "Backtracking through TFI's History," which examined cultural "flashpoints" dating to Berg's leadership and context of the 1960s (Amsterdam 2010a); a four-part series entitled "The Word of God," with theological justifications for doctrinal revisions (Fontaine 2010c); and "Blueprint for the Future," with redefinitions of discipleship and community (Amsterdam 2010b). It would be an understatement to say that members were bewildered by the Reboot documents, in particular their announcement of extensive doctrinal revisions and the dismantling of TFI's communal society model (Shepherd & Shepherd 2013: 79). Members were accustomed to major directional changes and periodic organizational restructuring. The Reboot, however, diverged from previous "revolutions" implemented within the bounds of TFI's high-commitment model of discipleship and communalism. In addition, the Reboot's disassembling of the organizational structure appeared antithetical to the evangelistic and congregational-building objectives upon which the change journey was premised (Amsterdam 2009b). The collective impact of the Reboot documents constituted in effect the deconstruction of TFI's ideology, religious practice, and shared values of the previous four decades. This section briefly outlines the revisionism introduced in the Reboot documents to belief, culture, and worldview, and explores the convergence of factors that led to the profound change introduced.

Doctrinal Revisions

The transition to a fundamentally different model of religious community necessitated significant revisions to TFI's theology to accommodate a redefinition of discipleship and religious practice that would align with its new objectives of growth and social relevance. This level of revisionism represented, as per Barker's definition, a reinterpretation of the movement's orthodoxy and orthopraxy to something recognizably different from the movement's original raison d'être (Barker 2013: 2–3). The most significant doctrinal revisions introduced included the affirmation of the authority of the Bible over TFI writings; the redefinition of TFI's leadership from a prophetic role to a minimally directional role; and the reinterpretation of the role of corporate prophecy.

Doctrinal revisionism introduced at the Reboot was premised on the establishment of two cornerstone principles: First, that the Bible was the authoritative Word of God, whereas TFI writings, previously considered the contemporary expression of God's Word, were redefined as "inspirational writings." Second, that the movement's doctrine was limited to core beliefs expressed in its Statement of Faith, while extrabiblical teachings and new revelation were relegated to a category termed "additional teachings." Members were expected to accept and affirm the doctrine expressed in the Statement of Faith – most of which aligns with evangelical orthodoxy – and were free to retain or disregard teachings outside that body of doctrine (Amsterdam 2010a; Fontaine 2010d). The movement's core doctrinal foundation as expressed in its Statement of Faith sustained minor modifications at the Reboot, whereas the majority of extrabiblical teachings based on revelation and prophecy that proliferated in the internal writings were removed from circulation and no longer considered part of TFI's canonical writings.

Corporate prophecy, a prominent feature of Maria's leadership and previously accorded authoritative status, represented a formidable obstacle to the recontextualization of TFI's theology. The extensive volume of published prophecies, largely presented as direct guidance from Jesus, unequivocally affirmed TFI's historic definitions of high-commitment world-rejecting discipleship and communal lifestyle. Most corporate prophecies published prior to the Reboot were out of step with the new theological understanding for discipleship and unsustainable in the post-Reboot context, which required their careful redefinition as time-contextual messages (Fontaine 2010b; Borowik 2013: 21–22). The Reboot's reinterpretation of corporate prophecy as temporal-contextual, and the diminishment of its role, inevitably raised the question as to whether previously published prophecy espousing absolute truths and discipleship expectations now abandoned had been false, misinterpreted, or erroneous. How were members to reconcile previous dogma and practice, deemed core to their Christian discipleship and special calling, with this fundamental redirection that ultimately represented a deconstruction of the movement's distinct identity and, by extension, members' personal identities? To accommodate these contradictions, acknowledgements were made that prophecy is not infallible and direction received in prophecy should not have been rigidly institutionalized or literally interpreted (Amsterdam in Fontaine 2010b). Maria also acknowledged and apologized for the burden and pressure that previously published prophecy had placed on the membership and the difficulty in reconciling previous demands and expectations articulated therein to the new context of the Reboot.

> Some of the concepts you staked your faith on that are now changing have shaped your life or had permanent outcomes that weigh into your future, or that of your loved ones. . . . We are deeply sorry if any of you are struggling or hurting, or feeling disadvantaged in any way now that we are experiencing so much change, or if the changes in our discipleship standard and requirements seem to place your past sacrifices and decisions in question. (Fontaine 2010b)

The Family's Law of Love doctrine was likewise reviewed in anticipation of the Reboot, in particular its controversial application to sexual sharing between consenting adult members regardless of marital status. Although the validity of the Law of Love doctrine and its allowance for sexual relations between members was ratified in principle at the Reboot, sexual sharing practices were significantly deemphasized and reconceptualized from doctrine to personal lifestyle choice (Fontaine 2010a). The Loving Jesus doctrine was recast at the Reboot as a metaphorical representation of the intimate spiritual relationship that Jesus desires with His followers, while sexual applications and any writings referring to this practice were removed from TFI's canon (Fontaine 2010c). Theologically, the revisions introduced at the Reboot repositioned TFI's beliefs in closer alliance to mainstream Christian orthodoxy while marginalizing the majority of TFI's heterodox doctrines and extrabiblical revelation, which in effect represented a relinquishment of its exclusivist truth claims. The Family's extensive library of publications dating from 1968 to 2010 was removed from circulation at the Reboot pending a review process to identify writings consistent with Reboot definitions of doctrine. Previous practices, dating to the early 1970s, of publishing writings with extrabiblical revelation designated "members only" and prohibited from sharing with outsiders, was discontinued at the Reboot. Any future publications would need to align with TFI's Statement of Faith and be outsider-friendly so that the writings could be freely shared with non-members, with a view to fostering an inclusive culture conducive to congregation-building and expanded membership.

Deconstructing the Culture

TFI's religious world was constructed on the understanding of discipleship as an all-encompassing commitment that required abandoning secular pursuits, burning bridges to members' past lives and social networks, and forging new bonds within the Family. From its early days, the movement was organized as a set-apart society, "God's revolution for this hour and day" with an elite role in the Endtime (Berg 1986b). Berg envisioned the Family as a form of godly utopian society, free from the ills of materialism and capitalism, where resources would be pooled for the benefit of all, and believers would commit their lives to reaching the world with the salvation message. The practice of communalism was understood to be instrumental for living out TFI's vision for true Christianity and members' calling as revolutionary disciples (Fontaine & Amsterdam 2004).

The changes introduced at the Reboot essentially deconstructed TFI's communitarian culture and collectivist ideology, representing a "180 degree shift" from its historic emphasis on the subordination of personal pursuits to TFI's communal and missional activities, to affirmations of the primacy of self-determination and personal autonomy (Shepherd & Shepherd 2013: 80).

In a Reboot document titled "Lifestyle," the movement's forty-year understanding of communalism as the early church model for discipleship was reinterpreted as a lifestyle choice, resulting in the dissolution of the communal society model that had been central to the perpetuation of its belief system (World Services 2010a). Cultural norms previously deemed imperative to maintaining boundaries of separation from the System were disavowed, including the discouragement of property ownership and secular employment, proscription of public and higher education, and disassociation with denominational Christianity. The movement's leadership and board structure were discontinued, thereby dismantling the framework for community gatherings or coordination of missionary endeavors.

The rationalization given for the deconstruction of TFI's communal society emphasized individualistic themes of personal choice and self-determination, encouraging members in the language of popular culture to "pursue your dreams" and "reach for the stars" (Amsterdam 2010b; Simon 2019). The post-Reboot TFI was reimagined as "a place of empowerment" for individuals, to "infuse members with inspiration and confidence to enact their dreams and plans for God" (Amsterdam, 2010b). As a whole, the Reboot documents intentionally shifted TFI's historic ideology from collectivist goals compatible with TFI's previous communal society model to endorsements of personal autonomy for each member to pursue God's personalized will in their new self-styled form of discipleship. This change in focus to personal empowerment and individualized discipleship represented a diametric shift in worldview and deconstruction of members' previous self-understanding as highly committed Christians with a unique calling and shared identity within a radical Christian community (Borowik 2018: 69–70).

The transition from a communal society model to a minimalist approach for membership centered in personal responsibility necessitated the annulment of hundreds of requirements and theological and pragmatic norms institutionalized in TFI's Charter. Only a handful of membership requirements were retained, including the submission of a monthly report and monetary offering, acceptance of TFI's Statement of Faith, and participation in evangelism. The rebooted Charter was reduced from a document of 310 pages to 30 pages, evidence of the extent of revisionism introduced at the Reboot (The Family International 2020).

Revising the Worldview

Prior to the Reboot, TFI had contended with varying degrees of internal tension in reconciling its dichotomous worldview that espoused both fundamentalist world-rejection and world-engagement for the purpose of evangelism.

Peter noted that the Reboot would transcend previous revolutions because of the "shift in the philosophy of the Family as a movement" that it represented (Amsterdam 2010c). A core philosophical redirection of the Reboot was its departure from TFI's historic "Christ against culture" ideology, previously central to its identity as disciples called out of an ungodly world and its rejection of corrosive influences of the world. The Reboot sought to pivot to a world-engaging philosophy and remove obstacles to success in evangelism, including unconventional and idiosyncratic lifestyle practices, and to reduce tension with denominational Christianity and society at large. A reversal of perspectives previously considered essential to the preservation of TFI's religious world was introduced, including engagement in secular activities such as employment and public education, although these perspectives had begun to slowly shift prior to the Reboot due to the realities of growing numbers of departing second-generationers and the need to facilitate their transition to society (Fontaine 2009).

The departure from the world-rejecting philosophy that had informed TFI's ideology from its early Jesus People Movement days called into question the movement's historic worldview. Berg's (and later Maria's) writings had claimed that the disciples were an elite class of Christians entrusted with revelatory spiritual truths and a special calling for the Endtime due to their high level of consecration to God and separation from the world. Berg intentionally disavowed the institutionalization of the movement or attempts to gain acceptance and popularity or growth in numbers, which he attributed to the perceived compromised state of denominational Christianity (Berg 1970d). The stated goals of the Reboot to contemporize the movement and its message and improve TFI's public image to pave the way for growth, influence and success diverged significantly from Berg's original vision (Amsterdam 2010a). The movement's emphasis on new member recruitment had diminished over the previous two decades, due in part to the realization that TFI's radical form of Christianity would not be attractive to most people. As priorities shifted to church growth and evangelism, it became evident that new strategies would be required to generate success, as well as to address the growing dissatisfaction of the second generation with TFI's insular boundaries. However, this new approach of modernizing the movement for evangelistic purposes stood at odds with the internally directed focus of previous retrenchment campaigns and the "reluctance to relinquish distinctive spiritual claims and moral identity" (Shepherd & Shepherd 2005: 68). This tension was resolved in corporate prophecies that declared that due to the success of previous retrenchment and recommitment campaigns, members were now spiritually prepared for the ushering in of a new era of success in its missionary endeavors (Fontaine & Amsterdam 2007).

Prophecies published from 2006 to 2008 also declared that the movement would overcome controversial legacy issues to experience popularity and membership growth and would expand its circle of influence exponentially (Borowik 2022: 210–11).

For the movement to implement long-term strategies for congregation-building and membership growth, TFI's foundational understanding of an imminent timeframe for the Endtime would need to be addressed. The expectation of the fulfilment of the biblical apocalypse within members' lifetime had weighed heavily in past organizational and evangelistic strategies. As a result, Chancellor noted that "the singular task was to get as many people saved as possible," which resulted in the movement being "highly mobile, and generally not geared toward the spiritual development and care of converts" (Chancellor 2005: 30–31). In 2009, Peter broached the topic of a possible delay in the Second Coming of thirty to fifty years or more as a change in construct needed to facilitate the implementation of long-term organizational strategies for missional success at the Reboot (Fontaine & Amsterdam 2009b). While this recontextualization of the Endtime was not framed as a change in doctrinal position, it represented a significant departure from TFI's foundational world-view and the lens through which current events and cultural trends were viewed. Berg's writings were laced with interpretations of political happenings and contemporary issues and the role these might play in ushering in the final seven years of world history, as well as theologizing to attempt to assign moral meaning to political and social events. This quest to construct theories as to how events of the day might fit into an imminent Endtime scenario became embedded within TFI's culture, giving rise to a quasi "conspiracy theory" subculture among a subset of members and former members who have pre-served Berg's legacy and continue to maintain expectations of an impending apocalypse (Fontaine 2020b; Amsterdam 2021).

Why the Reboot?

The scope of change unveiled at the Reboot introduced sweeping revisions of TFI's doctrine, culture, and worldview, as well as new ideological principles incompatible with its previous belief system. Prior to the Reboot, the movement had proved resourceful in adapting to changing situational contexts through periodic reorganizations and revising or annulling aspects of its belief system and practice. However, the Reboot took the unprecedented step of distancing the movement from elements of its religious world core to its identity, thereby posing the risk of destabilization and dissolution, a risk leadership frankly acknowledged:

> People have commented that they're not sure the Family will survive the change journey. It's true; there is that possibility. Conversely, the Family might not survive if we were to continue as we have been. ... We consider this a make-or-break moment for the Family. (Amsterdam 2010c)

This expression of concern for the Family's future in advance of the implementation of the Reboot gives rise to the question: Why the Reboot? What factors or countervailing forces were at work to produce an abrupt deconstruction and reinterpretation of elements of its religious world previously considered immutable? In retrospect, the convergence of numerous issues can be identified at work in the changes ushered in at the Reboot. The coming of age of the second generation and their demands for modernization and desire to legitimately pursue non-missionary careers, coupled with the realities of increasing numbers of second-generationers abandoning the movement, called into question the viability of TFI's insular practices. Prophecy published in the writings to address internal problems, demanding heightened levels of commitment and compliance to a growing body of discipleship norms, fostered a sense of weariness and dissatisfaction among the members (Fontaine 2010b). The aging of the first generation and the delay in millennial expectations would require long-term strategies for the care of the elderly not previously contemplated. The insurmountable burden of stigma and controversy due to legacy issues, coupled with the lack of appeal or relevance of TFI's exclusivist truth claims and lifestyle to potential converts, were not conducive to members' effectiveness in building mission works and financial stability (Borowik 2022: 211–12).

It had become apparent in the years leading up to the Reboot that historic practices of separation from the world had hampered members' ability to develop networks from which they might recruit new members and effectively engage in evangelism (Bainbridge 2002: 171; Amsterdam 2010c). The development of complex esoteric doctrine, coupled with an unconventional lifestyle and controversial sexual sharing practices, rendered the movement increasingly foreign to outsiders. Hard choices had to be made regarding exclusivist doctrines and anomalous practices that were inhibiting church growth objectives and financial stability. Socially radical beliefs and practices that sought to accentuate TFI's distinctiveness from conventional Christianity would have to be revised to lessen ingroup/outgroup boundaries and develop a message that would resonate with contemporary audiences (Borowik 2013: 19–20). Likewise, the movement's focus on the indoctrination and preservation of the second-generationers as the "hope of the future" (Fontaine 2000) would have to shift to gaining and discipling congregational members.

By the mid-1990s, second-generationers represented two-thirds of the membership, and a significant number of these were young adults. Their socialization and care had taken precedence over recruitment, a natural progression given that by the mid-1980s, recruitment rates had declined due to the "shrinking pool of potential recruits" from the counterculture era willing to experiment with alternative lifestyles, and TFI's forsake-all ideology and high level of movement-societal tension (Bromley 2013: 254). While the second generation were unquestionably a catalyst for change, they did not compensate for the decline in new member recruitment, nor did they offset TFI's defection rate (Bainbridge 2002: 171). A substantial percentage of this demographic came of age in the late 1990s and began to challenge aspects of the belief system and chafe at the restrictive boundaries in place and expectations that they would adhere to TFI's worldview and belief system. As an incremental rate of "born intos" began to disaffiliate by the early 2000s, boundaries between current and former members became increasingly untenable, due to familial ties and the strong subcultural bonds between second-generationers, regardless of membership status. It likewise became apparent that the future vitality of the movement could not depend solely on second-generation members.

Corporate prophecy published from 1996 to 2005 in defense of isolationist cultural practices and the preservation of TFI's exclusivist truth claims tended to contextualize the disaffiliations of second-generationers in spiritualized terms and as cautionary tales (Fontaine 2003; van Eck Duymaer van Twist 2015: 108–11). As the leadership increasingly grappled with concerns that the youth would be drawn away by their former member peers, strongly worded prophecies were channeled to affirm TFI's singular calling and place in Christianity and, by extension, that of the second generation, which required compliance to its high-commitment model of discipleship (Fontaine 2010b). Over time, it became evident by the growing numbers of disaffiliations that this was not a sustainable strategy considering the second generation's contextual and experiential differences from the first generation; a new approach was needed to "synchronize the direction and culture with their context and vision" (Fontaine & Amsterdam 2009b).

The incorporation of the second generation into leadership positions provided a platform for them to legitimately challenge boundaries on behalf of their peers and assert their desire for change and modernization. As a result, numerous accommodations were introduced in the 2000s to contemporize the culture, notably the allowance for contemporary music styles, art, comics, and fictional works. The publications of the 2000s became increasingly populated with spiritual heroes and villains that mirrored the superhero genre of popular culture, as well as magical powers, and supernatural keys and incantations reminiscent of the iconic *The Lord of the Rings* and *Harry Potter* fantasy series (see Figure 5). The Family International's sexual sharing practices, accorded renewed emphasis for

Figure 5 Artwork published in the *Good News*, a TFI publication, depicting spiritual powers and beings, published in 2005. Courtesy of the Family International.

the second generation in the late 1990s, provided a counterpoint to the hook-up and party culture of contemporary society (Borowik 2022: 210). Greater emphasis was placed on high school education and previous rhetoric condemning higher education and secular employment was significantly moderated, as the leadership acknowledged the reality that not all second-generationers would remain in the movement (Amsterdam 2003). Notwithstanding these accommodations, lingering presuppositions that children born into the movement had a special destiny with the Family hampered the movement's development of effective transition strategies for the inevitability of second-generationers opting for a secular lifestyle (Fontaine & Amsterdam 2009b).

The widespread integration of digital technology in the communal homes by the late 1990s introduced new avenues for exposure to other worldviews and secular perspectives for second-generationers eager to appropriate new technologies. Despite efforts to curb unfettered Internet access and spiritualized warnings of the dangers of the Internet, second-generationers increasingly engaged in boundary-permeating forays online, where they could interact with secular worldviews and with their former-member peers (Barker 2005: 76–77; Borowik 2018: 68). Exposure to external sources of information fostered comparisons of TFI's communal lifestyle, beliefs, and evangelism with successful Christian ministries, and the realization that these were largely out of step with modern society. Outsider perspectives became increasingly evident in organizational strategies, as for example in writings calling for new approaches to evangelism that incorporated secular strategies for success from popular authors such as Collins and Porras of *Built to Last: Successful Habits of Visionary Companies* (Amsterdam 2008b). Prophecy increasingly reflected the seepage of elements of prosperity gospel principles, including spiritual strategies for success and financial growth, the wielding of spiritual power for healing, and "naming and claiming" biblical promises for spiritual empowerment and prosperity (Jones & Woodbridge 2011: 15–19).

The writings from 2006 onward gradually shifted from the previous understanding of TFI as a persecuted minority with a countercultural calling to the pursuit of missional success, financial growth, influence, and overcoming TFI's negative public image to gain public acceptance and effectively engage with contemporary audiences (Amsterdam 2008a). By 2009, it had become evident that elements of TFI's culture and belief system were incompatible with these objectives and would have to be revised or discarded:

> Maria and I had to honestly admit that much of the Family's culture, methods, membership requirements, lifestyle restrictions, and mindsets were simply not bringing forth the success and growth we are all looking for. To realize our goals, we must change Family context, Family culture, Family rules, and attitudes and mindsets. (Amsterdam 2010c)

While the aging of first-generation members was not addressed in the Reboot documents, Peter acknowledged the issue in advance of the Reboot as an impending reality that would have to be discussed shortly thereafter (Amsterdam 2009b). The issue of an estimated 1,800 members simultaneously reaching retirement age within a decade or becoming incapable of keeping up with the demanding pace of the homes had not been seriously contemplated or previously addressed (Barker 2011: 8–9). The logistics of caring for a large cohort of elderly members and the financing of the communal homes, which would place an enormous burden on second-generationers and their children, doubtless factored into the dissolution of the communal society model (Barker 2011: 9–11). Shortly after the Reboot, a series of measures were introduced for the benefit of the older cohort (aged from mid-50s to mid-60s) to provide a one-time pension (a token gesture given the movement's limited financial means) and information on employment options and pensions in their countries of origin (Amsterdam 2011b).

In conclusion, the convergence of numerous factors and processes worked in tandem to precipitate the deconstruction of TFI's religious world and the profound revision of its theology, culture, and worldview. The doctrinal modifications introduced, coupled with the disassembling of the movement's organizational structure, represented a fundamental shift from TFI's intensely communalist culture to individualized discipleship and personal autonomy. The Reboot proved to be a definitive redirection in TFI's trajectory and potentially its final "revolution," as is explored in the next section.

5 Rewriting the Narrative: The Post-Reboot Virtual World of the Family International

The inauguration of the Reboot in 2010 with its deconstruction of vast swathes of TFI's doctrine and countercultural worldview represented an ideological reversal of belief and practice of the previous four decades, which Barker termed a "radical deradicalization" of the movement (Barker 2016: 419). The dismantling of the communal society model, a diametric shift from TFI's historical collectivist ideology, gave rise to the global migration of thousands of members to their native countries and a protracted process of identity renegotiation in their reintegration into conventional society. While many members remained on their mission fields, most essentially reinserted themselves into society and pursued employment or conventional forms of Christian ministry, while others undertook higher education to develop new careers. Within two years of the Reboot, the majority of communal homes had disbanded, the adult membership had declined by 32 percent, and frameworks for community and mission collaboration had become limited to periodic grassroots initiatives (Borowik 2017: 116).

As the groundwork was being laid for the Reboot in 2009, Peter and Maria acknowledged that "building a strong sense of community" would be "crucial to the future of the Family" (Fontaine & Amsterdam 2009b). The Reboot documents envisioned the implementation of a localized framework with facilitators to foster community and missional collaboration, with a projected timeline for its institution of 2011 (World Services 2010b). The proposed framework mirrored the loose-knit organizational structure of the Fellowship Revolution implemented in 1981 after the Reorganization Nationalization Revolution (RNR) of 1978. Numerous parallels can be traced between the Reboot and the

RNR, at which time Berg likewise dissolved the leadership structure, proclaimed a new era of personal autonomy, and delimited membership requirements to monthly reporting, tithing, and evangelism (Berg 1978b). However, the Reboot diverged significantly from the RNR in the dissolution of the communal society model, which historically served as the organizational framework for community for the movement's geographically dispersed membership. The success of the post-RNR Fellowship Revolution in recreating a vibrant community can be attributed in large part to the communal home model upon which it was built, unlike the post-Reboot TFI which lacked a viable framework for reconstructing community.

The failure to establish a community framework post-Reboot proved to be a contested point among the membership, which Peter addressed periodically, and most comprehensively in 2013, at which time he affirmed that a new structure would not be enacted in the foreseeable future (Amsterdam 2013a). In the absence of official mechanisms for community, the post-Reboot TFI unexpectedly evolved into an amorphous networked community with little formal structure beyond its online presence. Several websites were developed at the Reboot to reconfigure TFI's religious world online, including two websites for devotional publications: Directors' Corner (directors.tfionline.com) for Peter's and Maria's writings and Anchor (anchor.tfionline.com), a venue for publishing revised versions of pre-Reboot TFI writings, articles submitted by members, and resources from mainstream Christian authors, theologians, and apologists. While several other websites were developed for the membership, interactive social media platforms were not introduced, thus rendering much of TFI's post-Reboot digital world unidirectional with little provision for members to socially interact and recapture a sense of belonging.

By and large, members have either embraced or adjusted to TFI's current model or discontinued their membership. In some cases, the connection is purely cultural or nostalgic, and their participation in TFI and its mission work is minimal (Borowik 2017: 115–16). Membership has been in decline since 2010 at an average rate of nearly 11 percent per annuum. From a community of 5,400 adult members in ninety countries in 2009, with a transnational structure and membership extending three generations, by December 2021 TFI's membership had decreased to 1,410 members of eighty nationalities residing in seventy-four countries (TFI Services 2022). The Family International's income through tithes and offerings has also diminished at an average annual rate of nearly 7 per cent, necessitating the periodic discontinuation of services (Amsterdam 2019a). In 2009 TFI reported that 2,239 members were second-generation adults, representing 32 percent of the population, whereas in 2021, approximately 325 second or third-generationers remained, a loss of 85 percent of this demographic since the Reboot (TFI Services 2022). Of the 77 percent current first-generation members, as of December 2021, 42 percent were in their sixties and 22 percent in their seventies (TFI Services 2022). The attention of many members in this aging demographic necessarily has been diverted from missionary activities to medical issues, financial stability, family matters, and caring for elderly relatives (Barker 2011: 18–19).

The post-Reboot TFI has faced significant challenges in fostering movement vitality, member retention, and community cohesion in its transformation to online religion. This section considers the aftermath of the deconstruction and revisionism introduced at the Reboot and the post-Reboot reconstruction of TFI's belief system, identity renegotiation, and virtual reimagination of its community.

Reconstructing the Family International's Religious World Online

Throughout TFI's history, the movement had successfully maintained a cohesive subculture, due in large part to its sophisticated communication networks, despite the dispersion of its communities in scores of nations with great linguistic diversity (Shepherd & Shepherd 2007b: 241). In-house publishing mechanisms and communications systems were developed early on for the dissemination of publications and collection of monthly reports and tithes. The Family's writings, which included a wide array of publications from the official "Word of God" Letters to childrearing publications, educational, and missional resources, were central to the construction and reinforcement of the movement's subcultural identity and the socialization of its worldview within and across the communal homes. Novel Internet-based technologies were explored and integrated early on to facilitate the dissemination of its membership publications and to foster community. From the mid-1990s onward, TFI effectively navigated these new virtual spaces and innovatively refashioned digital technologies to further its evangelistic mission and build internal communication networks. By the early 2000s, Internet technologies had become increasingly central to the movement's administration, dissemination of Family writings, and community cohesion.

TFI's flagship website, www.thefamilyinternational.org, was launched in 1995 as an early new religion homesteader on the Web, followed by its Spanish counterpart in 1997, a Japanese version in 1998, and subsequently local versions in many languages. In 1997, the first members-only password-protected community website was created, which hosted prayer boards, interactive community spaces, and original in-house resources, including artwork, music, and homeschooling publications. By 2001, all TFI publications, previously printed at in-house printing centers and disseminated by mail, had been digitized and archived in a digital library. The Family International's monthly reporting system was transitioned to an online platform and an internal email system was adopted utilizing adaptations of encryption programs to protect these from outside scrutiny, a paramount concern due to the controversial nature of a number of the writings and the government interventions of the 1990s (Borowik 2018: 67).

The Family's integration of digital technologies from 1995 onward was pivotal to its post-Reboot transformation to online religion. In anticipation of the Reboot, websites were developed to integrate administrative and member services to online platforms. In 2013, an online community website was created, TFI Online (portal.tfionline.com), to compensate for the lack of mechanisms for in-person community (see Figure 6). TFI Online utilizes the movement's signature approach of adapting Internet technologies through the creation of a public interface and a members' interface to serve the dual purposes of advancing its public presence and preserving its internal religious world. The majority of post-Reboot TFI publications are accessible to the public through TFI Online, which offers subscription options to nonmembers, in keeping with the determination to reach a wider audience outside the

Figure 6 TFI Online provides a portal to the latest content published online and features a public interface and a members' interface. Screen capture published with permission from the Family International.

limited circle of its membership. Its members' interface, protected by encryption systems, strives to preserve the sense of community previously central to TFI membership and foster a degree of engagement in spaces where members can post want-ads and share prayer requests and news of their mission works (Borowik 2018: 68).

The Family International's post-Reboot online transformation has proven effective insofar as the publishing and dissemination of the movement's writings and mission resources are concerned, as well as its outreach to the public with its deradicalized Christian message. Nevertheless, the movement has struggled post-Reboot to reconstruct a shared identity for its members in solely virtual spaces, raising the question as to how effectively collective identities may be constructed, negotiated, and sustained in purely virtual environments (Lövheim 2013: 41). Prior to the Reboot, TFI had a rich tradition of religious worship, featuring original worship songs and prayer, and the nearly daily assembling of the homes for devotional services, as well as periodic inter-community worship gatherings on a local and regional basis.

The authenticity of disembodied community in technologically constructed spaces has been the subject of debate as to whether the Internet spawns impoverished forms of community or can generate innovative and vibrant forms of engagement (Campbell 2005: xvi; Bainbridge 2017: 89). The advent of COVID-19 broadened the scope of this debate, as many religious communities experimented with digital technologies to recreate religious ritual and community in online spaces during lockdowns (Bhambra & Tiffany 2021). Innovative online platforms were adopted by many churches in 2020 to adaptively respond to pandemic closures, featuring options for worship and community, including streamed religious services with interactive chat rooms and online spaces for social networking and real-time prayer, and virtual places for Bible study groups (Shellnut 2020). Bhambra and Tiffany's research indicated that notwithstanding the compensatory gains obtained by the integration of dynamic and interactive digital tools for religious worship, devotees nonetheless were fatigued by "one-sided worship" online and yearned for the horizontal spaces of in-person community (Bhambra & Tiffany 2021). In TFI's case, digital platforms for worship and religious services have not been leveraged to compensate for the lack of in-person community; rather, the use of digital technology has typically mirrored previous vertical patterns as dissemination mechanisms for TFI's writings or articles, with limited options for interactive engagement. The lack of digital platforms for community-building or horizontal social engagement has limited the extent of members' virtual networking experience or their ability to assemble for worship as an online community.

In the absence of democratized spaces for interactive social engagement, members and former members have created their own community spaces through Facebook groups, blogs, Skype, and other social media forums. Previous boundaries etched between members and former members have virtually disintegrated within many of these forums, insofar as these social networks are centered in shared experiences or nostalgia. These residual forms of community that have organically emerged at best represent a sort of imagined community, fashioned around common history, beliefs, and subcultural bonds that would be largely incomprehensible to outsiders. However, this sort of online community subjectively reshaped around personalized networks and past experiences bears little resemblance to TFI's previous identity as a movement with a sense of destiny, centered in its radical interpretations of Christianity (Borowik 2018: 74–81).

Post-Reboot Doctrinal Revisionism

In light of the extensive doctrinal revisionism introduced at the Reboot, an exhaustive reappraisal was undertaken of the tens of thousands of TFI publications and multimedia resources produced from 1968 to 2010 to determine whether these would be retained, revised, or discarded. Standards were established for republishing pre-Reboot publications to ensure that writings preserved would be amenable to Reboot objectives of limiting the doctrine to core beliefs expressed in TFI's Statement of Faith and relevancy to a wider audience of congregational-style members (Fontaine 2010b). The nearly 2,900 Mo Letters penned by Berg from 1968 to 1994 underwent a rigorous review process post-Reboot, resulting in the preservation of excerpts of 450 of his letters. The majority of Maria's writings, which were largely prophetic and revelatory in nature, were not reintegrated into TFI's official library in their original format. Editorial license was granted to the administrators of Anchor for the excerpting and revising of pre-Reboot writings, thereby providing a venue for the recontextualization of previous writings to align with TFI's post-Reboot doctrine and worldview. As of 2022, adapted versions of over 250 of the 900 missives published by Maria from 1995 to 2010 have been recycled through Anchor (Borowik 2022: 212–13).

The TFI Online Library website, accessible only to members, currently houses nearly 33,000 files, including pre- and post-Reboot writings, publications for children and teenagers, resources for evangelism, and music productions. The Family International's prolific collection of nearly 150 original music albums was largely reinstituted post-Reboot, whereas little of TFI's signature artwork, previously featured in its internal publications and evangelistic posters, has been reinstated. Several websites were created post-Reboot to archive legacy cultural and nostalgic artifacts, notably the Children of God website (childrenofgod.com) which hosts a collection of some 5,000 photos, publications, news articles, and musical productions from the COG era. The Family International's signature monthly magazine, *Activated,* is archived on its public website (activated.org), which received 507,000 unique visitors in 2021 (TFI Services 2022).

The post-Reboot review process of TFI's former library of publications served to officially remove from TFI's canon any writings incompatible with the doctrinal stances adopted at the Reboot (Fontaine 2010b). Although the Reboot's revision of TFI's doctrine significantly realigned the theology with Christian orthodoxy, in theory it also made allowance for the publication of extrabiblical additional teachings and new revelation post-Reboot, insofar as these did not contradict biblical principles (Fontaine 2010c). However, pre-Reboot theological innovations have rarely been republished, and extrabiblical teachings removed from circulation have not been reinstated or re-contextualized to date, nor have new extrabiblical teachings been published. In practice, Peter's post-Reboot writings have been devoted overwhelmingly to imparting mainstream evangelical teachings in numerous series devoted to Bible studies, indicative of the shift to Christian orthodoxy. His book, *The Heart of it All: Foundations of Christian Theology,* teaches standard evangelical theology without striving to reconcile these teachings with pre-Reboot hetero-dox doctrinal interpretations (Amsterdam 2019b). "Living Christianity," a thirty-one-part series on the Ten Commandments published from 2018 to 2020, provides affirmations of the moral law of the Ten Commandments, a significant redirection from Berg's writings, which were absolute in their insistence that the Ten Commandments "are no more to the followers of Jesus" (Berg 1984a). In the preface to this series, Peter bridged this incongruence by reaffirming previous Family teachings that Christians are not required to live according to Old Testament law, while proposing that the Ten Commandments provide "a framework for addressing moral and ethical standards for Christians" (Amsterdam 2018). Although this recontextualization of the Ten Commandments was not presented as a new doctrinal position, it represented a significant diver-gence from core beliefs previously articulated in TFI's Statement of Faith.

The Family's Law of Love doctrine and associated heterodox sexual ethics were premised entirely on the understanding that the Ten Commandments had been superseded by Jesus' command to love God and love neighbor as self. This doctrine was understood as inherently encompassing the moral code of the Ten Commandments – excluding prohibitions for adultery, which fell to the realm of progressive revelation. While the Reboot document "Applying the Law of

Love" ratified in principle Berg's Law of Love doctrine and associated sexual applications, no mention has been made in post-Reboot writings of previous heterodox sexual practices or Berg's antinomian justifications for these (Fontaine 2010a). To the contrary, Peter's series on the Ten Commandments would appear to uphold biblical prohibitions of adultery and affirm the sanctity of marriage. In 2019, the "Applying the Law of Love" document was redacted and retitled "Marriage, Divorce and Child Support," effectively excising any references to previous antinomian sexual practices or ethics from TFI's official canon and library.

The publishing of corporate prophecy, predominant in Maria's writings from 1996 to 2009, has greatly diminished post-Reboot. The brief prophecies published in nearly 100 of Maria's 370 post-Reboot articles have rarely contained corporate instruction. Ongoing revelation, reaffirmed at the Reboot as a core TFI belief, has not occurred, and extrabiblical teachings or Endtime interpretations are rarely visible in post-Reboot writings. Corporate prophecy and new revelation clearly have been superseded by the contemporary devotional and minimally directional style adopted for TFI writings post-Reboot (Fontaine 2010d). As a notable exception, in 2020 Maria published corporate prophecies containing spiritual direction regarding the COVID-19 pandemic (Fontaine 2020a). In 2021, Peter published a response to members' speculations and questions as to whether the pandemic was an apocalyptic sign, as well as conspiracy theories surrounding the COVID vaccine, in which he dismissed such theories as lacking in biblical support (Amsterdam 2021).

In summary, the doctrinal revisionism introduced at the Reboot clearly has been institutionalized, and in fact has extended beyond what was envisioned at the time – extrabiblical teachings previously prevalent in the literature have not been reinstituted, new revelation has not occurred, while new affirmations of Christian orthodoxy have been introduced. However, the question remains as to how effectively the Reboot's doctrinal mega-shift has been integrated into members' personal worldviews and belief systems, and whether a set of documents issued in 2010 have effectively overwritten forty years of indoctrination, first under Berg's leadership and subsequently via corporate prophecy. From interviews conducted in 2015 and the perusal of social media of members and former members, it is evident that great diversity exists in people's current ideological positions, with some continuing to embrace Berg's writings or later eras of TFI's history, while others have abandoned TFI teachings or joined mainstream churches (Borowik 2018: 70–79). Online counternarratives and published interviews seem to indicate that a number of second-generationers have deconstructed their faith and consider themselves "nones" or nominal Christians or have abandoned Christianity (van Eck Duymaer van Twist 2015: 175, 186–88).

Renegotiating Identity, Culture, and Community

Kanter's observation of the importance that communitarians place on their uniqueness and coherence, and their high degree of awareness of what their community stands for and their role in history provides an apt description of TFI's pre-Reboot subcultural identity (Kanter 1972: 52–53). Despite the inherent challenges of a controversial worldview and complex lifestyle, evolving internal and external pressures and financial precarity, the shared environment within the Family communes provided coherence and purpose, and fostered vibrant interpersonal relationships and a deep sense of belonging. The precipitous unraveling of TFI's communal society produced extensive upheaval that affected virtually every aspect of members' lives, far surpassing the impact of doctrinal revisions which members could variously integrate into their worldview or disregard. The difficulties TFI has faced post-Reboot in reconstructing a shared identity, community, and purpose underscore the vital role communalism played in the maintenance of TFI's religious world and its longevity in the face of significant challenges and opposition.

The Reboot's departure from TFI's collectivist ideology had the unintentional consequence of calling into question both the movement's identity and members' personal identities. While members welcomed overall the concepts of personal autonomy and individualized conceptualizations of discipleship, many struggled with the loss of community and the values upon which their lives had been premised (Borowik 2018: 74–75). The results of a 2011 membership poll that elicited a 67 percent response rate indicated that 94 percent of participants considered that "it was important for them to be in community with likeminded TFI members" (Amsterdam 2011a). In response to questions and concerns expressed by members regarding the lack of agency for community development and the sense that the movement was in decline, Peter produced several webcasts in 2013 that addressed questions such as: "Why TFI?" "Why Be a TFI member?," and "Is TFI a Dying Movement?"

> A lot of people have written us and asked us, "Why was it so needed, why did we have to do that, where are those things today, that's what I really miss, the camaraderie." . . . These changes really got to the heart of the Family, to who we were, to how we did things, to our culture, to just everything, and it was very massive. And it caused us to lose some things that we had – some of the camaraderie, the living together, the closeness.
>
> (Amsterdam 2013a)

Peter pointed to several countervailing factors to the implementation of the new framework for community articulated in the Reboot documents, in particular members' aversion to previous styles of leadership and lifestyle differences that had evolved post-Reboot. His webcast further proposed that members would have to take the initiative to mobilize and enact community-building efforts, whether through orchestrating in-person gatherings or virtual meetups through Skype and Facebook. Formal fellowship meetings since the Reboot that occur periodically in different parts of the world or local informal gatherings represent unofficial initiatives organized by members and may include committed members, former members, and nominal members, with little distinction between participants (Borowik 2017: 115–16). In the absence of access to mechanisms for community, Peter proposed that members consider joining local churches or work with other unchurched Christians or start up their own house church if their community needs could not be met with other TFI members (Amsterdam 2013a). While this approach would have been virtually unheard of in the past, the Reboot's reversal of TFI's stance of separation from conventional Christianity served to deconstruct previous sharply dichotomous *them* and *us* boundaries. Whereas members had little exposure pre-Reboot to mainstream Christian teachings and read almost exclusively TFI publications that resonated with TFI's interpretations of Christian doctrine, the Reboot introduced a new openness to mainstream Christian teachings. However, it is unknown to what extent members and former members have adjusted their worldviews to discard previous negative conceptualizations of conventional Christianity or joined mainstream churches or ministries.

Given TFI's reinvention as a virtual network, the geographic dispersal of members, and the reordering of their lives and commitments, it seems unlikely that TFI would have the means to introduce new frameworks for community in the future. The cultural displacement produced by the Reboot was profound, resulting in fragmentation and identity crises, which required a redefining of reality for members as they reintegrated into a world they had abandoned decades earlier. Some members framed the magnitude of displacement they experienced with immigrant analogies expressive of the angst of separation from their culture and community (Borowik 2018: 70). Although members have embraced personally empowering aspects of the Reboot, many have grappled with the separation from people with whom they shared a common set of beliefs and practices, the disaffiliation of their second-generation children, and reconciling their life commitments to a movement in decline (Barker 2011:19; Borowik 2018: 71–73). Unquestionably, a wide diversity of experience exists in people's personal reinventions post-Reboot and reintegration into society; by and large, many appear to have effectively transitioned from TFI's communal society and support system and have developed new social networks. However, as Shepherd and Shepherd's research indicated, this positive adaptive response has not been universal, and some longtime members became disillusioned and felt betrayed by what they perceived to be "an incomprehensible repudiation of practices and beliefs they thought were inviolable and binding revelations from the Lord" (Shepherd & Shepherd 2013: 83).

The Family International's subcultural identity as radical Christians and a "spiritual elite under the guidance of prophets, directly in contact with Jesus, to facilitate his imminent Second Coming" (Shepherd & Shepherd 2013: 90) has not been reconstructed post-Reboot, nor has a special calling been accorded to members. Interviews with members and former members in 2015 indicated that the concept of membership, previously central to their identity, held little relevance post-Reboot, and some expressed uncertainty as to whether their spouses considered themselves members (Borowik 2018: 70). In the absence of a new construct to foster coherence and recapture the sense of unique purpose, identity reconstruction efforts have been further complicated by the aging of members and decline in membership. Most second-generationers, who provided much of the impetus for the modernization and deradicalization introduced at the Reboot, disaffiliated from TFI shortly thereafter. While a number of members have continued to maintain vibrant mission and charitable works in developing nations, many members are less engaged in evangelistic activities due to their work and family responsibilities (Borowik 2018: 71; Barker 2022: 27).

Online Challenges to TFI's Post-Reboot Reinvention

As noted in Section 3, the repositioning the of the cult wars in online environments introduced a challenging platform of identity management for new religious movements such as TFI in the struggle for religious tolerance and public representation. The permanence of potentially delegitimizing information published on the Internet, a forum that arguably has proved more amenable to countermovement propagation of information, coupled with the ease of dissemination, have created problematic new dynamics for new religions in the public realm (Cowan 2004: 266–68). Johnson's research on "The Fall of Mars Hill Church in Seattle" argues that online public testimonies of former members, coupled with social media and archival practices, combined to disrupt founder Mark Driscoll's charismatic authority and catalyzed the dissolution of the Mars Hill megachurch (Johnson 2020: 121–22). The role of the production and circulation of online counternarratives in the precipitous dissolution of

Mars Hill bears some resemblance to the online struggle TFI has faced in its efforts to overcome past controversy and reinvent itself as a contemporary Christian movement.

Prior to the Reboot, TFI had vacillated for a decade between innovatively adapting to new realities emergent in a digital age and the preservation of its radical roots and insular religious world. However, as the cult wars increasingly were repositioned in online spaces, it became evident that the social media dynamics of a Web 2.0 world required new strategies to overcome negative profiling of TFI online, which largely focused on legacy issues since the Rodriguez murder–suicide in 2005. Concerted efforts were made post-Reboot to reinvent TFI's public image, including the deployment of public websites and wikis, a social media presence, search engine optimization, and the posting online of public acknowledgments and apologies addressing legacy issues. However, the stigmatization of the movement on the Internet proved to be a formidable barrier to its envisioned transformation in the public sphere as a legitimate Christian movement. Despite the Reboot's efforts to eradicate contentious beliefs and practices and lessen tension with society and mainstream Christianity, the controversy surrounding TFI has not abated. In fact, public censure of the movement arguably has intensified in recent years, largely due to the proliferation of second-generation counternarratives embedded in the milieu of contemporary cancel culture.

The reinvention of TFI's public persona and efforts to legitimize the movement increasingly lacked a context in the face of the fragmentation of TFI's collective identity post-Reboot, membership decline, and the movement's metamorphosis as a virtual network with no brick-and-mortar presence. Prior to the Reboot, TFI had proved adept at managing adversity and rationalizing it within its worldview as a persecuted church; members manifested a high degree of resilience in the face of conflict and opposition insofar as TFI sustained a coherent community with a shared belief system and worldview. However, the Reboot's deconstruction of TFI's identity as a countercultural movement in a state of resistance to the dominant cultural matrix proved disruptive to the "magical coherence" of its "sacred universe" (Paden 1994: 55). In the absence of a distinct subcultural identity, in-person community and tangible support system, TFI post-Reboot increasingly lacked a construct for the rationalization of the movement's stigmatization in the virtual court of public opinion. In addition, the propagation of legacy issues online placed members and former members alike in the precarious position of negotiating potential damage to their personal reputations and future prospects in the process of reconstructing their lives. The discovery or disclosure of affiliation with TFI, whether past or present, could introduce risks to people's careers, employment, or charitable works due to contemporary dynamics of public shaming and censorship (Pew Research Center 2021; Tidwell & Falinski 2022). Interviews with members and former members indicated that many have opted to not disclose their current or past affiliation with TFI to strategically manage damaged identity and the stigma attached to cult membership, due to fears of discrimination, potential job loss, disruption of familial relations, and the unrelatability of their past experiences to outsiders (Borowik 2018: 78–79).

In conclusion, the struggle TFI has faced in its reinvention as a virtual religious community serves to highlight the complexities of effectively reconfiguring religious community, ritual, and shared identity in purely online environments. As of 2022, core objectives of the Reboot remain unrealized, and the lack of a new organizational model to foster community and reverse trends of declining membership, coupled with post-Reboot ambiguities in the movement's identity and purpose have impeded its evangelistic and congregation-building aspirations. At this stage in TFI's history, it seems unlikely that efforts at reinvigorating the community would be met with the affirmative response of past reorganizations, given the diversity in members' post-Reboot experiential, situational, and geographical contexts. The realities of an aging population – including Maria and Peter, now in their 70s – the lack of a cohesive community, and the online delegitimization of the movement, place in question the movement's ability to reconstruct a subcultural identity that will survive into the future (Shepherd & Shepherd 2013: 93–94).

6 Conclusions

Wessinger proposed that new religions may be conceptualized as "arenas for theological and social experimentation" that emerge from "human creativity and capacity for religious expression," providing spiritual meaning and social connection (Wessinger 2005). The Children of God's journey from its early fundamentalist Jesus People beginnings to the social construction of a new religious movement, to its current metamorphosis as a deradicalized online community provides evidence of the dynamic nature of new religions, and their potential to adapt and innovate. In Wright's analysis, the movement's versatility and adaptiveness to cultural pluralism and organizational and generational change in its restructuring from a hippie countercultural group to a multiethnic, decentralized missionary organization contributed significantly to its survival (Wright 1994: 123–27). Bainbridge's extensive survey of TFI members in 2002 indicated that despite the hardships of TFI's itinerant lifestyle, controversy and opposition, and the challenges of numerous people cohabiting under one roof, the movement represented a coherent way of life for members (Bainbridge 2002: xiii). The interactive spaces afforded by TFI's communal society model for religious expression and shared identity and purpose were central to the movement's ability to evolve and to "thrive in its own way" throughout four decades (Melton 1997: 61).

Studies of the COG ranging from its early history to TFI's latter days as a communal movement have offered various observations regarding the sustainability of the movement and its potential to endure into the future. In 1972, Enroth and colleagues argued that it was "a safe assumption" that the COG would undergo the splintering the authors deemed typical of groups with authoritarian structures (Enroth et al. 1972: 53). In 1987, Wallis posited that the movement "was all too likely" to descend into chaos and collapse upon Berg's death due to the disruption of his charismatic authority (Wallis 1987: 89). Van Zandt proposed in 1995 that "neither an immediate disintegration nor a gradual shift to the status of an established sect" was "in the cards" but rather the movement would continue for an extended period as an insular, cohesive movement, limited only by its ability to retain its children as members (Van Zandt 1995: 132). Melton suggested that having weathered the court cases of the early 1990s and accommodated to the demands of the dominant culture, the Family's "future appears to be stable" as it "moves to develop a more settled congregation-oriented lifestyle" (Melton 1997: 61–2). In 2002, Bainbridge proposed that the Family was well-positioned to innovate into the future, while noting several counterfactuals to its growth and membership retention (Bainbridge 2002: 170-3). A few years later, Chancellor noted that having survived the "death of the prophet" and come to terms with the loss of many second-generationers, TFI's energy and mission focus could carry the movement into the future (Chancellor 2005: 39). Shepherd and Shepherd suggested with caution that by 2009 TFI had "successfully instituted organizational forms and mechanisms for sustaining a religious way of life likely to persist for generations to come," assuming it continued to adaptively respond to new contingencies (Shepherd & Shepherd 2010: 210). Clearly the movement's resilience and accommodative response in the face of the government interventions of the 1990s, the introduction of democratization processes under the Charter as a legal–rational organizational document, and its integration of the second generation into leadership appeared to bode well for its future. This raises the question as to how the movement, which in Barker's analysis seemed at the turn of the century to be "going from strength to strength" could appear to be "on the brink of extinction" two decades later (Barker 2020:106).

The Reboot introduced elements that would appear to dispense with the remaining tension with society and facilitate the movement's evangelistic objectives, deconstructing previous *them* and *us* boundaries and exclusive truth claims, while adopting more conventional definitions for Christian service and discipleship. The process that led to the Reboot was grounded in principle on the premise of success in TFI's evangelistic mission, gauged in terms of converts, influence, financial stability, and expansion of congregational circles of membership (Amsterdam 2010c). Historically the movement's criteria for success had not been posited on growth or influence, but rather on fulfillment of its salvific mission and commitment to its calling as a radical Christian movement for the Endtime. In the process of analyzing TFI's history, culture, and organizational model prior to the Reboot, it became evident that much of its worldview was rooted in its early history and millennial expectations and would have to be realigned with the movement's future-focused strategies and objectives. Due to concerns of preserving Berg's legacy and organizational model, strides of modernization and development introduced after his death had been continuously counterpoised by restrictive measures to preserve elements of the movement's worldview from its countercultural roots (Amsterdam 2010a). In "Backtracking through TFI's History," Peter systematically deconstructed elements of Berg's worldview rooted in the 1960s countercultural moment that had lingered on in the writings and ideology (Amsterdam 2010a). Peter's analysis echoed Wilson's observations of how movements can become "frozen in certain postures," visible in TFI's case in the carrying over of the cultural imprint of features of the 1960s counterculture within TFI's belief system and organizational model, which had become increasingly irrelevant and could eventually lead to failure (Wilson 1987: 44; Amsterdam 2010c).

Previous sections identified numerous factors that led to the comprehensive revisionism and reorganization introduced at the Reboot and the subsequent decline in membership, representative of a complex interaction of endogenous and exogenous factors (Wright et al. 2020: 16). Various issues likewise conspired in the dissolution of TFI's historic communal society model, in particular the departure of growing numbers of second-generationers, the aging of the first generation, and the perception that TFI's communal lifestyle was not relatable or socially relevant to outsiders (Borowik 2018: 79). Leadership's focus on the preservation of radical features of the movement deemed immutable clashed with the realities of everyday communal life on the ground and fundraising imperatives that required an engaging public presence, and proved increasingly unsustainable. A growing body of esoteric mystical revelation with extrabiblical truth claims further impeded members' outreach programs and new member recruitment as the belief system became increasingly complex and incomprehensible to outsiders. The movement's "prophet on the mountain" model with a leadership body in seclusion that rarely engaged in person with the membership was likewise incompatible with attempts to modernize the organization and attain legitimacy as a contemporary religious movement. Lastly, the murder–suicide perpetrated by Ricky Rodriguez gave rise to a renewed wave of negative media coverage that has persisted to the present, notwithstanding reforms introduced in the mid- to late-1980s and the favorable court decisions of the early 1990s (Bainbridge 2017: 98–100).

Twelve years after the Reboot, the future viability of the movement in its current amorphous and individualized configuration is uncertain, considering the year-over-year decline in membership and revenues and the lack of a system for new member recruitment to revitalize the movement. Most members would appear to have effectively reintegrated into society and moved on in new directions for their lives, likely with both regrets and happy memories, though others have struggled substantially in the transition process (Barker 2020: 112–13). A successorship plan was not instituted at the Reboot, nor was the creation of a viable board or leadership structure contemplated to carry the movement forward into the future. In the absence of a new organizational framework to foster community and missional collaboration, the Reboot's objective of contemporizing TFI to achieve its evangelistic objectives – one of the main rationales presented for disassembling the communal society model – has not produced the envisioned outcomes. Members interviewed in 2015 expressed a sense of gratification with the personal autonomy and self-styled discipleship model introduced at the Reboot, but also lamented the loss of community and manifested disappointment with the outcomes of the Reboot:

> As a movement, in the form and format as it was, [the Reboot] ended it. The whole idea is that it would resurrect, that it would Reboot in another fashion. I think it has, but just not what we expected. We expected it to still be a cohesive movement, and I feel like it's not. (Ashley in Borowik 2018: 71)

The assumption woven throughout TFI's pre-Reboot writings was that the Letters were the primary source for the movement's cohesion and stability, enabling the implementation of periodic reorganizations without destabilizing the movement. However, the cultural disruption that occurred in the aftermath of the dissolution of the communal society model serves to highlight the central role that communalism played in the longevity of the movement and shared identity of members. Members resided together and held experiences and narratives in common; meaning and identity were co-constructed and reinforced in everyday life, which served to forge a vibrant and resilient culture that transcended nationality and geographic location (Borowik 2022: 220). The grassroots social media groups and networks that spontaneously emerged on a horizontal level after the dismantling of the communal homes provide evidence of members' and former members' quest to recapture a sense of belonging and identity and to share in nostalgic remembrances (Barker 2011: 19). However, social interactions in these virtual spaces are largely centered in pre-existing relationships and previous experiences rather than shared beliefs or religious commitments, which may diverge significantly since the Reboot, thus limiting their ability to compensate for TFI's previous community.

In 2013, Peter responded to members' disappointment with the aftermath of the Reboot and concerns that the movement was dying by introducing a new narrative for success and flourishing:

> Something I've heard quite a bit lately, and I'm pretty sure you've heard it too, is that the Family is a dying movement or it's dead or it's on its last leg. The Family is not dead, the Family's not dying. It's alive in you. ... The things that really make the Family alive, God's Spirit, His movement, His desire to win souls, His inspiration, His word, the life that He gives us, that's not dead at all. (Amsterdam 2013b)

As members have attempted to make sense of the post-Reboot version of TFI, some have speculated on the anticipated approach of the Endtime as a rationale for the disassembling of the organizational structure (Borowik 2018: 71). Members' identification with the belief in the imminence of the biblical apocalypse and the search for signs of the ushering in of the final seven years of world have persevered, and in some cases gained new momentum, despite the Reboot's recontextualization of its imminence. Affirmations of an impending Endtime and speculation on contemporary world events through an apocalyptic lens are visible on websites, blogs, podcasts, and in books published by members and former members. This revitalized focus on the imminence of the Endtime echoes Wright and colleagues' proposal that new religious movement decline may be reinterpreted in spiritualized terms or as "evidence for the approaching of the end of times" (Wright et al. 2020: 13–4).

Having set in motion a process of essentially "dismantling a religious tradition" (Robbins 2014: 2) that previously shaped members lives and identity, can TFI carry on as a movement into the future within the limitations of online religious engagement while still providing relevance and spiritual compensators for its members? Notwithstanding the decline in membership, the movement continues to maintain a robust presence online and hosts dynamic websites with regular new content that attracts a substantial following for a Christian network with fewer members than the average megachurch. In 2021, TFI's websites received more than 2,000,000 unique visitors from 212 nations and 22 languages, who viewed nearly 3,000,000 pages of content (TFI Services 2022). The Family International's leveraging of online spaces and digital technologies for evangelistic purposes has empowered the movement to attain to what decades earlier would have seemed extraordinary in the dissemination of its Christian message to a global audience, and hardly a sign of decline.

The Family International's social construction of a vibrant online presence in the face of membership decline raises questions regarding the ways in which definitions of the decline and demise of movements may be reinterpreted within virtual spaces. The virtualized version of TFI may model to some extent what Bainbridge has proposed as "online residualism," whereby decline may not necessarily lead to the demise of significant features of the movement as residues of its culture may persist through its "online survival" (Bainbridge 2017: 89). The online version of post-Reboot TFI appears to be sufficient to provide continuity for members and for former members who access the public interface; nevertheless, it seems unlikely that this will produce new momentum or revitalization. The extent to which collective identity and ritual engagement may be authentically sustained in purely virtual environments is also uncertain, as indicated by the sense of disconnection and disengagement that some members expressed, as well as ambivalence toward TFI due to its lack of relevance to members' contemporary lives (Borowik 2018: 80). In addition, the weight of stigma and public hostility the movement has endured in the digital public square due to legacy issues has impeded TFI's efforts at reinventing itself as a contemporary movement that has addressed past error and shed radical features.

The integration of digital technologies and online spaces unquestionably has introduced new dynamics to the ways in which religious belief, identity, and community are practiced, as well as a contentious platform of negotiation for religious movements. Bainbridge proposed that new religions are more likely to survive in societies with less evolved information technologies, where the movements are better able to protect their religious worlds and preserve their official histories, while avoiding the repercussions of damaging information that can be instantly uploaded and widely disseminated in cyberspace (Bainbridge 2017: 100). The ability of new religious movements to survive and thrive in the future may be severely tested in the current environment of online counternarratives, cancel culture and social exclusion, and infotainment media's pursuit of sensationalistic stories to gain subscribers and "hits." The quest for religious tolerance and the free exercise of religion may prove to be what Lucas referred to as an "uphill battle for survival" for new religions in the twenty-first century due to "a constellation of social forces that can repress, critique, persecute, and battle new and minority religions" (Lucas 2004: 281–82).

The Family International's transformation from a radical communal movement to a deradicalized virtual community offers insights into the ways in which new religious movements may be socially reconstructed in online spaces, and how belief, identity, and culture may be profoundly altered or reconfigured in the process. The Family International's digital reinvention also highlights the novel dimensions cyberspace has opened for new religions to perpetuate their beliefs, culture, and history in cyberspace and proclaim their religious message, even into their twilight years. The online challenges TFI has faced post-Reboot sheds light on new dynamics at work in the struggle for survival and legitimacy of new religious movements as online and offline worlds increasingly interface, raising questions regarding the future viability of religious innovation and experimentation. The Family International's history is indicative of the potential of new religions for innovation and resilience, as evidenced by its creation of a coherent subculture and cohesive community, grounded in its high-commitment style of Christianity, that endured for five decades in the face of numerous challenges, opposition, and controversy. The movement has continuously evolved and remapped aspects of its religious world as its members established communes in over ninety nations, embraced ethnic diversity, adapted to local cultures, and published its distinctive message in numerous languages. In what appears to be the Family International's final chapter, the movement and its members continue to share its unique brand of Christianity through the dissemination of the Gospel message in twenty languages and on multiple websites, and humanitarian and charitable programs across the globe.

Bibliography

Amsterdam, P. 1995. *Moving Forward: The Need for Change*. Internal document. The Family.

Amsterdam, P. 2003. *Charter Amendments 2003*. Internal document. The Family.

Amsterdam, P. 2006. *Training for the Winning Offensive*. Internal document. The Family International.

Amsterdam, P. 2007. *The Family's History, Policies, and Beliefs regarding Sex*, pts 1–3. Internal documents. The Family International.

Amsterdam, P. 2008a. *A Professional Lifestyle for the Offensive*. Internal document. The Family International.

Amsterdam, P. 2008b. *Got Strategy? Creating a Strategy Plan for the Offensive*. Internal document. The Family International.

Amsterdam, P. 2009a. *Beyond Boundaries*, pt 3, *Second Generation Leave-Takers*. Internal document. The Family International.

Amsterdam, P. 2009b. *The Change Journey*. Internal document. The Family International.

Amsterdam, P. 2010a. *Backtracking through TFI History*. Internal document. The Family International.

Amsterdam, P. 2010b. *Blueprint for the Future*. Internal document. The Family International.

Amsterdam, P. 2010c. *Change Journey Manifesto*. Internal document. The Family International.

Amsterdam, P. 2011a. *A Snapshot of the TFI Member Poll*. (May). Internal document. The Family International.

Amsterdam, P. 2011b. *Update on Care of the Elderly Program*. (June). Internal document. The Family International.

Amsterdam, P. 2013a. "Community and Structure." YouTube video (March 11). The Family International. www.youtube.com/watch?v=haDuXp37nTY.

Amsterdam, P. 2013b. "Is TFI a Dying Movement?" YouTube video (February 18). The Family International. www.youtube.com/watch?v=bpF65y7nAgo.

Amsterdam, P. 2018. "Living Christianity," pts 1–31. The Family International. https://portal.tfionline.com/en/pages/living-christianity/.

Amsterdam, P. 2019a. *Renewing our Commitments*. (January). Internal document. The Family International.

Amsterdam, P. 2019b. *The Heart of it All: Foundations of Christian Theology*. The Family International. https://portal.tfionline.com/en/pages/the-heart-of-it-all/.

Amsterdam, P. 2021. "Signs of the Times and Current Events." (May). Internal document. The Family International.

Bainbridge, W. S. 2002. *The Endtime Family: Children of God.* Albany, NY: State University of New York Press.

Bainbridge, W. S. 2017. *Dynamic Secularization: Information Technology and Tension between Religion and Science.* London: Springer.

Bainbridge, W. S. 2020. *The Social Structure of Online Communities.* Cambridge: Cambridge University Press.

Barker, E. 1986. "Religious Movements: Cult and Anticult Since Jonestown." *Annual Review of Sociology* 12: 329–46.

Barker, E. 1995a. "Plus Ça Change . . ." *Social Compass* 42, no. 2: 165–80.

Barker, E. 1995b. "The Scientific Study of Religion? You Must Be Joking!" *Journal for the Scientific Study of Religion* 34, no. 3: 287–310.

Barker, E. 1998. "Standing at the Cross-Roads: The Politics of Marginality." In D. Bromley, ed., *The Politics of Religious Apostasy: The Role of Apostates in the Transformation of Religious Movements*, 75–93. Westport, CT: Praeger.

Barker, E. 2005. "Crossing the Boundary: New Challenges to Religious Authority and Control as a Consequence of Access to the Internet." In M. T. Højsgaard & M. Warburg, eds., *Religion and Cyberspace*, 67–85. New York: Routledge.

Barker, E. 2011. "Ageing in New Religions: The Varieties of Later Experiences." *Diskus* 12: 1–23. http://eprints.lse.ac.uk/50871/.

Barker, E. 2013. "Revision and Diversification in New Religions: An Introduction." In E. Barker, ed., *Revisionism and Diversification in New Religious Movements*, 15–30. Farnham: Ashgate.

Barker, E. 2016. "From the Children of God to the Family International: A Story of Radical Christianity and De-radicalising Transformation." In S. J. Hunt, ed., *Handbook of Global Contemporary Christianity: Movements, Institutions, and Allegiance*, 402–21. Leiden: Brill.

Barker, E. 2020. "Denominationalization or Death? Comparing Processes of Change within the Jesus Fellowship Church and the Children of God aka The Family International." In M. Stausberg, S. A. Wright & C. M. Cusack, eds., *The Demise of Religion: How Religions End, Die, or Dissipate*, 99–118. London: Bloomsbury Academic.

Barker, E. 2022. "What Did They Do about It? A Sociological Perspective on Reactions to Child Sexual Abuse in Three New Religions." In B. Singler & E. Barker, eds., *Radical Transformations in Minority Religions*, 13–38. London: Routledge.

Barrionuevo, A. 2022. "Superstar DJ Alok Leaned on Unpaid Ghost Producers to Create His Brazilian Bass Hits." *Billboard* (January). www.billboard.com/pro/alok-dj-ghost-producers-sevenn-brazilian-bass/.

Berg, D. 1968. "Our Declaration of Revolution." *Mo Letter* no. 1336. The Children of God.

Berg, D. 1970a. "Colonisation." *Mo Letter* no. C. The Children of God.

Berg, D. 1970b. "General Epistle to Leaders." *Mo Letter* no. 24. The Children of God.

Berg, D. 1970c. "I Gotta Split!" *Mo Letter* no. 28. The Children of God.

Berg, D. 1970d. "Quality or Quantity?" *Mo Letter* no. 23. The Children of God.

Berg, D. 1971a. "The Gypsies." *Mo Letter* no. 61. The Children of God.

Berg, D. 1971b. "Jesus People? Or Revolution!" *Mo Letter* no. 148. The Children of God.

Berg, D. 1971c. "Let My People Go." *Mo Letter* no. 144. The Children of God.

Berg, D. 1972a. "One Wife." *Mo Letter* no. 249. The Children of God.

Berg, D. 1972b. "Other Sheep." *Mo Letter* no. 167. The Children of God.

Berg, D. 1972c. "Survival." *Mo Letter* no. 172. The Children of God.

Berg, D. 1972d. "The 70-Years Prophecy of the End." *Mo Letter* no. 156. The Children of God.

Berg, D. 1972e. "The Great Escape!" *Mo Letter* no. 160. The Children of God.

Berg, D. 1973a. "40 DAYS! And Nineveh Shall Be Destroyed!" *Mo Letter* no. 280. The Children of God.

Berg, D. 1973b. "Bye, Bye, Pie!" *Mo Letter* no. 232. The Children of God.

Berg, D. 1973c. "New Bottles." *Mo Letter* no. 251. The Children of God.

Berg, D. 1973d. "The Goddesses." *Mo Letter* no. 224. The Children of God.

Berg, D. 1974. "Forsaking All." *Mo Letter* no. 314A. The Children of God.

Berg, D. 1975a. "Strange Truths." *Mo Letter* no. 360. The Children of God.

Berg, D. 1975b. "The Childcare Revolution!" *Mo Letter* no. 330B. The Children of God.

Berg, D. 1975c. "The Education Revolution." *Mo Letter* no. 371. The Children of God.

Berg, D. 1977a. "Our Declaration of Love." *Mo Letter* no. 607. Children of God.

Berg, D. 1977b. "Out of This World." *Mo Letter* no. 686. The Children of God.

Berg, D. 1978a. "The End-Time Witnesses." *Mo Letter* no. 707. The Children of God.

Berg, D. 1978b. "The Re-Organisation Nationalisation Revolution!" *Mo Letter* no. 650. The Children of God.

Berg, D. 1978c. "When I'm Gone." *Mo Letter* no. 706. The Children of God.

Berg, D. 1979. "Coming of Age!" *Mo Letter* no. 771. The Children of God.

Berg, D. 1980. "Yesterday's Children." *Mo Letter* no. 2348. The Family.

Berg, D. 1981a. "My Testimony!" *Mo Letter* no. 1177. The Family.

Berg, D. 1981b. "The Fellowship Revolution!" *Mo Letter* no. 1001. The Family.

Berg, D. 1982. "Face Up, Dress Up, Trim Up, Straighten Up!" *Mo Letter* no. 1202. The Family.

Berg, D. 1984a. "Amazing Grace! Free at Last!" *Mo Letter* no. 1968. The Family.

Berg, D. 1984b. "Sinless Sex! God's Sex Position." *Mo Letter* no. 1969. The Family.

Berg, D. 1984c. "When the Comet Comes!" *Mo Letter* no. 1770. The Family.

Berg, D. 1985. "No Such Thing as Bad Publicity." *Mo Letter* no. 2217. The Family.

Berg, D. 1986a. "The Revelation of the Antichrist." *Mo Letter* no. 2191. The Family.

Berg, D. 1986b. "We Are It!" *Mo Letter* no. 2222. The Family.

Berg, D. 1986c. "What If?" *Mo Letter* no. 2211–1. The Family.

Berg, D. 1988. "The Word, The Word, The Word!" *Mo Letter* no. 2484. The Family.

Berg, D. 1991. "Consider the Poor." *Mo Letter* no. 2755. The Family.

Berg, D. 1992. "Another Sign of the End!" *Mo Letter* no. 2827. The Family.

Bhambra, M. & Tiffany A. 2021. "From the Sanctuary to the Sofa: What COVID-19 Has Taught Us about Sacred Space." LSE Blog (April). https://blogs.lse.ac.uk/religionglobalsociety/2021/04/from-the-sanctuary-to-the-sofa-what-covid-19-has-taught-us-about-sacred-space/.

Borowik, C. 2013. "The Family International: Rebooting for the Future." In E. Barker, ed., *Revisionism and Diversification in New Religious Movements*, 15–30. Farnham: Ashgate.

Borowik, C. 2014. "Courts, Crusaders and the Media: The Family International." In J. T. Richardson & F. Bellanger, eds., *Legal Cases, New Religious Movements, and Minority Faiths*, 19–40. Farnham: Ashgate.

Borowik, C. 2017. "The Family International: The Emergence of a Virtual New Religious Community." In E. V. Gallagher, ed., *"Cult Wars" in Historical Perspective*, 108–20. New York: Routledge.

Borowik, C. 2018. "From Radical Communalism to Virtual Community: The Digital Transformation of the Family International." *Nova Religio* 22, no. 1: 59–86.

Borowik, C. 2022. "Digital Revisionism: The Aftermath of The Family International's Reboot." In B. Singler & E. Barker, eds., *Radical Transformations in Minority Religions*, 207–24. New York: Routledge.

Bradney, Anthony. 1999. "Children of a Newer God." In S. Palmer & C. Hardman, eds., *Children in New Religions*, 210–23. London: Rutgers University Press.

Bromley, D. G. 1998. *The Politics of Religious Apostasy: The Role of Apostates in the Transformation of Religious Movements*. Westport, CT: Praeger.

Bromley, D. 2013. "Changing Vision, Changing Course: Envisioning/Re-Visioning and Concentration/Diversification in NRMs." In E. Barker, ed. *Revisionism and Diversification in New Religious Movements*, 247–60. Burlington, VT: Ashgate.

Campbell, H. 2005. *Exploring Religious Community Online: We are One in the Network*. New York: Peter Lang.

Chancellor, J. D. 2000. *Life in The Family: An Oral History of the Children of God*. Syracuse, NY: Syracuse University Press.

Chancellor, J. D. 2005. "A Family for the Twenty-first Century." In J. R. Lewis & J. A. Petersen, eds., *Controversial New Religions*, 19–42. New York: Oxford University Press.

Chancellor, J. D. 2008. "The Family International: A Brief Historical and Theological Overview." *Sacred Tribes Journal* 3, no. 1: 5–32.

Clark, M. D. 2020. "DRAG THEM: A Brief Etymology of So-Called 'Cancel Culture'." *Communication and the Public* 5, nos. 3–4: 88–92.

Collins, J. C. & Porras, J. 1994. *Built to Last: Successful Habits of Visionary Companies*. New York: Harper Collins.

Cowan, D. E. 2004. "Contested Spaces: Movement, Countermovement, and E-space Propaganda." In L. L. Dawson & D. E. Cowan, eds., *Religion Online: Finding Faith on the Internet*, 255–72. New York: Routledge.

Cowan, D. E. & D. G. Bromley. 2008. *Cults and New Religions: A Brief History*. Malden, MA: Wiley-Blackwell.

Cresswell, J. 2022. "These Photos Explore the Lives of Women in and after Cults." Refinery29 (October). www.refinery29.com/en-gb/women-fleeing-cults-photo-series.

Davis, D. 1984. *The Children of God: The Inside Story*. Grand Rapids, MI: Zondervan Books.

Davis, R. & J. T. Richardson. 1976. "The Organization and Functioning of the Children of God." *Sociological Analysis* 37, no. 4: 321–39.

Dawson, L. L. 1999. "When Prophecy Fails and Faith Persists: A Theoretical Overview." *Nova Religio* 3, no. 1: 60–82.

Drakeford, J. W. 1972. *Children of Doom: A Sobering Look at the Commune Movement*. Nashville: Broadman Press.

Dunford, J. 1999. *Hartnett v. State of New South Wales: New South Wales Supreme Court*, 265. Sydney, Australia, 31 March.

Ellwood, R. S. 1973. *One Way: The Jesus Movement and Its Meaning*. Englewood Cliffs, NJ: Prentice-Hall.

Enroth, R., E. E. Ericson, & C. B. Peters. 1972. *The Jesus People: Old-time Religion in the Age of Aquarius*. Grand Rapids, MI: Eerdmans.

Eskridge, L. 2013. *God's Forever Family: The Jesus People Movement in America*. New York: Oxford University Press.

Fontaine, M. 1994a. *The Jonah Phenomenon!* Internal document. The Family.

Fontaine, M. 1994b. *Why We 'Preached Sex' in the Press Release Announcing Dad's Homegoing!* Internal document. The Family.

Fontaine, M. 1995a. *An Answer To Him That Asketh Us!* Internal document. The Family.

Fontaine, M. 1995b. *Mama's Love Story!*, pt 2. Internal document. The Family.

Fontaine, M. 1995c. *The Loving Jesus Revelation*, pts 1–7. Internal document. The Family.

Fontaine, M. 1995d. *State of the Nation '95!* Internal document. The Family.

Fontaine, M. 1998. *Living the Lord's Law of Love*, pts 1–12. Internal documents. The Family.

Fontaine, M. 2000. *Issues*, pt 4. Internal document. The Family.

Fontaine, M. 2001. *Be True to the Revolution!* Internal document. The Family.

Fontaine M. 2002. *Full Possession*. Internal document. The Family.

Fontaine, M. 2003. *Keep the Faith!* Internal document. The Family.

Fontaine, M. 2009. *Education for Life*. Internal document. The Family International.

Fontaine, M. 2010a. *Applying the Law of Love*. Internal document. The Family International.

Fontaine, M. 2010b. *God's Words for Today: Prophecy and Revelation*. Internal document. The Family International.

Fontaine, M. 2010c. *The Word of God: Yesterday, Today and Forever*. Internal document. The Family International.

Fontaine, M. 2010d. *God's Words for Today: A Living Faith*. Internal document. The Family International.

Fontaine, M. 2020a. "Conquering Fear with Faith: A Response to the Coronavirus Crisis." (April). The Family International. https://anchor.tfionline.com/post/conquering-fear-with-faith/.

Fontaine, M. 2020b. *Current Events: Speculations and Opinions* (October). Internal document. The Family International.

Fontaine, M. & P. Amsterdam. 2000. *The Way Things Really are in WS!* Internal document. The Family.

Fontaine, M. & P. Amsterdam. 2004. *Forward, Always Forward*. Internal document. The Family International.

Fontaine, M. & P. Amsterdam. 2007. *Liftoff!* Internal document. The Family International.

Fontaine, M. & P. Amsterdam. 2008. "An Open Letter of Apology to Current and Former Second-Generation Family Members." The Family International. www.myconclusion.com/apology-to-second-generation.html.

Fontaine, M. & P. Amsterdam. 2009a. "Letter of Apology from Karen Zerby (Maria) and Steve Kelly (Peter) to Former Members of the Family International (formerly the Children of God)." The Family International. www.myconclusion.com/apology-to-former-members.html.

Fontaine, M. & P. Amsterdam. 2009b. "The Future of The Family International: Establishing a Culture of Innovation and Progress." Paper presented at CESNUR Conference, Salt Lake City.

Greymoor, W. 2021. "Sex Cult Nun: Breaking Away from the Children of God, a Wild, Radical Religious Cult." *San Francisco Book Review*. https://sanfranciscobookreview.com/product/sex-cult-nun-breaking-away-from-the-children-of-god-a-wild-radical-religious-cult/.

Hunt, S. J. 2008. "Were the Jesus People Pentecostals? A Review of the Evidence." *PentecoStudies* 7, no. 1: 1–33.

Introvigne, M. 2000. "Moral Panics and Anti-cult Terrorism in Western Europe." *Terrorism and Political Violence* 12, no. 1: 47–59.

Introvigne, M. 2022. "Are Apostates Reliable? The Problem of Apostasy." *Bitter Winter* (January). https://bitterwinter.org/are-apostates-reliable-1-the-problem-of-apostasy/.

Isserman, M. & M. Kazin. 2000. *America Divided: The Civil War of the 1960s*. New York: Oxford University Press.

Johnson, J. 2020. "The Fall of Mars Hill Church in Seattle: How Online Counter-Narratives Catalyzed Change." In M. Stausberg, S. A. Wright & C. M. Cusack, eds., *The Demise of Religion: How Religions End, Die, or Dissipate*, 119–34. London: Bloomsbury Academic.

Jones, D. W. & R. S. Woodbridge. 2011. *Health, Wealth & Happiness: Has the Prosperity Gospel Overshadowed the Gospel of Christ?* Grand Rapids, MI: Kregel Publications.

Kanter, R. M. 1972. *Commitment and Community: Communes and Utopias in Sociological Perspective*. Cambridge, MA: Harvard University Press.

Lövheim, M. 2013. "Identity." In H. A. Campbell, ed., *Digital Religion: Understanding Religious Practice in New Media Worlds*, 40–56. New York: Routledge.

Lucas, P. C. 2004. "The Future of New and Minority Religions in the Twenty-first Century: Religious Freedom under Global Siege." In P. C. Lucas & T. Robbins, eds., *New Religious Movements in the Twenty-first Century: Legal, Political, and Social Challenges in Global Perspective*, 341–58. New York: Routledge.

MacDonald, A. & E. Stetzer. 2020. "The Lasting Legacy of the Jesus People: How an Unlikely, Countercultural Movement went Mainstream. *Talbot Magazine* (June). www.biola.edu/blogs/talbot-magazine/2020/the-lasting-legacy-of-the-jesus-people.

Meissner, L. 2015. LinkedIn profile. www.linkedin.com/in/linda-may-meissner-49086068/.

Meissner, L. 2016. "Linda Meissner on the Days of 'The Cross and the Switchblade' and the Jesus People Movement." www.youtube.com/watch?v=1s-d4lw1FP8.

Melton, J. G. 1985. "Spiritualization and Reaffirmation: What Really Happens When Prophecy Fails." *American Studies* 26, no. 2: 17–29.

Melton, J. G. 1997. *The Children of God: 'The Family'*. Salt Lake City: Signature Books.

Miller, T. 1999. *The 60s Communes: Hippies and Beyond*. Syracuse, NY: Syracuse University Press.

Miller, T. 2011. *The Hippies and American Values*. Knoxville: University of Tennessee Press.

Nash, N. C. 1993. "Argentines Say a Sex Cult Enslaved 268 Children." *New York Times* (September). www.nytimes.com/1993/09/03/world/argentines-say-a-sex-cult-enslaved-268-children.html.

NBC. 1971. "The Ultimate Trip." *First Tuesday*. Television documentary. 120 minutes.

Niebuhr, H. R. 1929. *Social Sources of Denominationalism*, 12th ed. New York: World Publishing Group.

Niebuhr, H. R. 1951. *Christ and Culture*. New York: Harper and Row.

Oubiña, A. F., J. I. Perez Burred & J. Bachs Estany. 1992. *Judgement in Cases 0160/92*. Provincial Court Barcelona. Spain, 21 May.

Paden, W. E. 1994. *Religious Worlds: The Comparative Study of Religion*. Boston: Beacon Press.

Palmer, S. J. (2011). "Rescuing Children? Government Raids and Child Abuse Allegations in Historical and Cross-Cultural Perspective." In S. A. Wright & J. T. Richardson, eds., *Saints under Siege*, 51–79. New York: New York University Press.

Pew Research Center. 2021. "Americans and 'Cancel Culture': Where Some See Calls for Accountability, Others See Censorship, Punishment." www.pewresearch.org/internet/2021/05/19/americans-and-cancel-culture-where-some-see-calls-for-accountability-others-see-censorship-punishment/.

Prack, H. E., A. Mansur, & D. Rudi. 1993. *Judgment in Case 81/89*. Federal Appeals Court of San Isidro, Province of Buenos Aires, Argentina, 13 December.

Richardson, J. T. 1982. "Financing the New Religions: Comparative and Theoretical Considerations." *Journal for the Scientific Study of Religion* 21, no. 3: 255–68.

Richardson, J. T. 1995. "Manufacturing Consent about Koresh." In S. Wright, ed., *Armageddon in Waco: Critical Perspectives on the Branch Davidian Conflict*, 153–76. Chicago: University of Chicago Press.

Richardson, J. T. 1999. "Social Control of New Religions: From 'Brainwashing' Claims to Child Sex Abuse Accusations." In S. J. Palmer & C. E. Hardman, eds., *Children in New Religions*, 172–86. New Brunswick: Rutgers.

Richardson, J. T. 2021. "The Myth of the Omnipotent Leader: The Social Construction of a Misleading Account of Leadership in New Religious Movements." *Nova Religio* 24, no. 4: 11–25.

Richardson, J. T. & R. Davis. 1983. "Experiential Fundamentalism: Revisions of Orthodoxy in the Jesus Movement." *Journal of the American Academy of Religion* 51, no. 3: 397–425.

Ruiz Nuñez, H. 1993. "Los Jueces No Deben Juzgar Pecados" [Judges Shouldn't Judge Sins]. *Revista Humor* (December), 27–28, Argentina.

Robbins, J. 2014. "How Do Religions End? Theorizing Religious Traditions from the Point of View of How They Disappear." *Cambridge Anthropology* 32, no. 2: 2–15.

Shellnut, K. 2020. "When God Closes a Church Door, He Opens a Browser Window." *Christianity Today* (March). www.christianitytoday.com/news/2020/march/online-church-attendance-covid-19-streaming-video-app.html.

Shepherd, G. & G. Shepherd. 2005. "Accommodation and Reformation in the Family/Children of God." *Nova Religio* 9, no. 1: 67–92.

Shepherd, G. & G. Shepherd. 2006. "The Social Construction of Prophecy in The Family International." *Nova Religio* 10, no. 2: 29–56.

Shepherd, G. & G. Shepherd. 2007a. "Grassroots Prophecy in the Family International." *Nova Religio* 10, no. 4: 38–71.

Shepherd, G. & G. Shepherd. 2007b. "The Family International: A Case Study in the Management of Change in New Religious Movements." *Religion Compass* 1, no. 1: 229–44.

Shepherd, G. & G. Shepherd. 2009a. "Prophecy Channels and Prophetic Modalities: A Comparison of Revelation in the Family International and the LDS Church." *Journal for the Scientific Study of Religion* 48, no. 4: 734–55.

Shepherd, G. & G. Shepherd. 2009b. "World Services in The Family International: The Administrative Organization of a Mature Religious Movement." *Nova Religio* 12, no. 3: 5–39.

Shepherd, G. & G. Shepherd. 2010. *Talking with the Children of God*. Chicago: University of Illinois Press.

Shepherd, G. & G. Shepherd. 2011. "Learning the Wrong Lessons: A Comparison of FLDS, Family International and Branch Davidian Child-Protection Interventions." In C. Jacobson & L. Burton, eds., *Modern Polygamy in the United States: Historical, Cultural, and Legal Issues*, 237–58. New York: Oxford University Press.

Shepherd, G. & Shepherd, G. 2013. "Reboot of The Family International." *Nova Religio* 17, no. 2: 74–98.

Shupe, A. & D. Bromley. 1994. *Anti-cult Movements in Cross-Cultural Perspectives*. New York: Garland Publishing.

Shupe, A. & J. K. Hadden. 1995. "Cops, News Copy, and Public Opinion: Legitimacy and the Social Construction of Evil in Waco." In S. Wright, ed., *Armageddon in Waco: Critical Perspectives on the Branch Davidian Conflict*, 177–202. Chicago: University of Chicago Press.

Simon, E. C. 2019. "This Author Wants You to Rethink 'Following Your Dreams'." *Repeller* (April). https://repeller.com/you-deserve-the-truth/.

Smith, C. 1998. *American Evangelicalism: Embattled and Thriving*. Chicago: University of Chicago Press.

Smithson, J., dir. 1994. *Children of God*. Television Documentary. 63 minutes.

Taylor, C. 2007. *A Secular Age*. Cambridge, MA: Harvard University Press.

TFI Services. 2022. "2021 Year-End Report." Internal document. The Family International.

The Family International. 2010. "Statement of Faith." www.thefamilyinternational.org/en/about/our-beliefs/.

The Family International. 2020. *Charter of the Family International*. https://portal.tfionline.com/en/pages/charter/.

Thomson, N., dir. 2007. *Children of God: Lost and Found*. Documentary film. 66 minutes.

Thussu, D. K. 2008. *News as Entertainment: The Rise of Global Infotainment*. Los Angeles: Sage.

Tidwell, S. & J. Falinski. 2022. "The Good, the Bad and the Dirty: Analyzing Cancel Culture and Its Effects." *The State News* (April). https://statenews.com/article/2020/09/a-look-into-cancel-culture?ct=content_open&cv=cbox_latest.

Tipton, S. 1982. *Getting Saved from the Sixties: The Transformation of Moral Meaning in American Culture*. Berkeley: University of California Press.

Trott, J. 1995. "History in the Making: Longhairs for Jesus." *Christian History Magazine*, Issue 48. https://christianhistoryinstitute.org/magazine/article/history-in-the-making-longhairs-for-jesus.

Van Eck Duymaer van Twist, A. 2015. *Perfect Children: Growing Up on the Religious Fringe*. Oxford: Oxford University Press.

Van Zandt, D. E. 1991. *Living in the Children of God*. Princeton, NJ: Princeton University Press.

Van Zandt, D. E. 1995. "The Children of God." In T. Miller, ed., *America's Alternative Religions*, 127–32. Albany, NY: SUNY Press.

Wallenstein, H. J. 1974. "Final Report on the Activities of the Children of God. Report Submitted to Louis J. Lefkowitz, Attorney General of the State of New York." New York: Charity Frauds Bureau.

Wallis, R. 1979. *Salvation and Protest: Studies of Social and Religious Movements*. New York: St. Martin's Press.

Wallis, R. 1981. "Yesterday's Children: Cultural and Structural Change in a New Religious Movement." In B. Wilson, ed., *The Social Impact of New Religious Movements*, 97–133. New York: Rose of Sharon Press.

Wallis, R. 1982. "The Social Construction of Charisma." *Social Compass* 29, no. 1: 25–39.

Wallis, R. 1984. *The Elementary Forms of the New Religious Life*. London: Routledge & Kegan Paul.

Wallis, R. 1987. "Hostages to Fortune: Thoughts on the Future of Scientology and the Children of God." In D. Bromley & P. E. Hammond, eds., *The Future of New Religious Movements*, 80–90. Macon, GA: Mercer University Press.

Wessinger, C. 2005. "New Religious Movements: An Overview." Encyclopedia.com. CENGAGE. www.encyclopedia.com/environment/ encyclopedias-almanacs-transcripts-and-maps/new-religious-movements-overview.

Wikipedia. 2022. "Wikipedia About." https://en.wikipedia.org/wiki/Wikipedia: About.

Wilson, B. R. 1987. "Factors in the Failure of the New Religious Movements." In D. G. Bromley & P. E. Hammond, eds., *The Future of New Religious Movements*, 30–45. Macon, GA: Mercer University Press.

World Services. 1987. "The Comet Comes!" The Family.

World Services. 1994. *Family Discipline Guidelines*. Internal document. The Family.

World Services. 2010a. "Lifestyle." Internal document. The Family International.

World Services. 2010b. "Structure and Services." Internal document. The Family International.

Wright, S. A. 1994. "From 'Children of God' to 'The Family': Movement Adaptation and Survival." In J. R. Lewis & J. G. Melton, eds., *Sex, Slander, and Salvation: Investigating the Family/Children of God*, 121–28. Stanford: Center for Academic Publication.

Wright, S. A. 1997. "Media Coverage of Unconventional Religion: Any 'Good News' for Minority Faiths?" *Review of Religious Research* 39, no. 2: 101–15.

Wright, S. A. 1998. "Exploring Factors That Shape the Apostate Role." In D. Bromley, ed., *The Politics of Religious Apostasy: The Role of Apostates in the Transformation of Religious Movements*, 95–115. Westport, CT: Praeger.

Wright, S. A. & S. J. Palmer. 2016. *Storming Zion: Government Raids on Religious Communities*. New York: Oxford University Press.

Wright, S. A., Stausberg, M. & Cusack, C. M. 2020. "How Religions End: Terms and Types." In M. Strausberg, C. M. Cusack & S. A. Wright, eds., *The Demise of Religion: How Religions End, Die, or Dissipate*, 13–30. London: Bloomsbury Academic.

Cambridge Elements ☰

New Religious Movements

Founding Editor

†James R. Lewis

Wuhan University

The late James R. Lewis was Professor of Philosophy at Wuhan University, China. He was the author or co-author of 128 articles and reference book entries, and editor and co-editor of 50 books. Most recently, he was the the general editor for the *Alternative Spirituality and Religion Review*, and served as the associate editor for the *Journal of Religion and Violence*. His prolific publications include *The Cambridge Companion to Religion and Terrorism* (Cambridge University Press, 2017) and *Falun Gong: Spiritual Warfare and Martyrdom* (Cambridge University Press, 2018).

Series Editor

Rebecca Moore

San Diego State University

Rebecca Moore is Emerita Professor of Religious Studies at San Diego State University. She has written and edited numerous books and articles on Peoples Temple and the Jonestown tragedy. Publications include *Beyond Brainwashing: Perspectives on Cultic Violence* (Cambridge University Press, 2018) and *Peoples Temple and Jonestown in the Twenty-First Century* (Cambridge University Press, 2022). She is reviews editor for *Nova Religio*, the quarterly journal on new and emergent religions published by the University of California Press.

About the Series

Elements in New Religious Movements go beyond cult stereotypes and popular prejudices to present new religions and their adherents in a scholarly and engaging manner. Case studies of individual groups, such as Transcendental Meditation and Scientology, provide in-depth consideration of some of the most well-known, and controversial, groups. Thematic examinations of women, children, science, technology, and other topics focus on specific issues unique to these groups. Historical analyses locate new religions in specific religious, social, politicial, and cultural contexts. These examinations demonstrate why some groups exist in tension with the wider society and why others live peaceably in the mainstream. The series highlights the differences, as well as the similarities, within this great variety of religious expressions. To discuss contributing to this series, please contact Professor Moore at remoore@sdsu.edu.

Cambridge Elements ≡

New Religious Movements

Lightning Source UK Ltd.
Milton Keynes UK
UKHW020622010223
416280UK00021B/307